YORKSHIRE BATTLEFIELDS

Yorkshire Battlefields

A GUIDE TO THE GREAT CONFLICTS ON YORKSHIRE SOIL 937-1461

GRAHAM BELL

Wharncliffe Books

First Published in 2001 by
Wharncliffe Books
an imprint of
Pen and Sword Books Limited,
47 Church Street, Barnsley,
South Yorkshire. S70 2AS

Copyright © Graham Bell 2001

For up-to-date information on other titles produced under the
Wharncliffe imprint, please telephone or write to:

> **Wharncliffe Books**
> **FREEPOST**
> **47 Church Street**
> **Barnsley**
> **South Yorkshire S70 2BR**
> **Telephone (24 hours): 01226 - 734555**

ISBN: 1-903425-12-3

A CIP catalogue record of this book is available from the
British Library

Printed in the United Kingdom by
CPI UK

CONTENTS

INTRODUCTION

Yorkshire Military History 43 AD - 937AD

The mighty Napoleon was once heard to declare, 'a nation's geography is its history'. What Napoleon said of the history of continental Europe (and he should know, having conquered most of it) could also be said of God's given country, Yorkshire.

No other county in England has seen so many large-scale combats; no other county has seen such slaughter through the ages. The reason for this unpleasant factor is quite simple: Yorkshire lies at the crossroads of England.

The county of Yorkshire is a natural funnel for armies to march through. Split in two by the Pennines, the roads in mainland Britain north and south are forced into a westerly and easterly route. Given the fact that the eastern part of these islands tended to be far more populous and fertile than the western, it was only natural those predatory armies should march up this war-corridor on their way to plunder and conquest. The fact that the county was unpleasantly near the Scottish border, meant that raiders from both north and south of the border, would from the times of the Romans, sweep north and south on pillaging expeditions and campaigns of slaughter.

This uncomfortable strategic position was compounded by another factor: the huge ocean inlet known as the Humber estuary. From the days of the later Roman Empire, this inlet of the North Sea has been an invasion route of Jutes, Angles, Saxons and Vikings who have used this waterway to invade, plunder and colonise Yorkshire. On two occasions, the destiny of mediaeval Europe was decided by troops sailing up the Humber to try to conquer the

Druids working the Britons up to oppose the landing of the Romans.

Saxon realm of England. The first ended in a victory which resulted in the development of a state that became the most centralised and powerful in Western Christendom; the second, though ending in victory, was only the prelude to a defeat in the south, the results of which would be a century or more of tyranny, savage oppression and cultural debasement for the losers.

The military history of Yorkshire, begins, oddly enough, with the landing in the south-east of the most effective killing machines in the history of the ancient world, the Roman legions, led by the eccentric Emperor Claudius, in 43AD.

Apart from a desire to gain glory by conquering a semi-mystic land regarded as containing a people who were one-half mad and the other half savage (an impression which, it seems, a large part of continental Europe still seems to hold) historians have been mystified as to why Claudius invaded the land of Britannia in the first place.

Regardless of the fears of his troops, the landing was successful, and the Roman Legions soon spread over the land bringing with them the inevitable accompaniment of the Roman Imperium: baths, bridges, theatres, Roman law. They also brought with them the less attractive elements of their culture: the savagery of the amphitheatre, crucifixion, and, perhaps the worst of all, the study of Greek and Roman

A Caledonian or Pict.

philosophy, which generations of scholars (this writer, alas, not excepted) have had to plough through.

Despite the heroism of the southern British tribes in opposing the Roman war machine, by 60AD, most of Britain south of the Trent was occupied. The revolt of Boudicca, (60-61 AD) was only a temporary setback, and by 74 AD, the Roman frontier had reached the River Tees. By this time, York had become the most important city north of the Trent. Its situation on the River Ouse, the fact that the Romans (inevitably) built a bridge over the river and the fact that it was the highest point of the Ouse a Galley could reach, made York a natural capital for the north. It was a legionary fortress from 70 AD, where the then governor of Britain, Petillius Cerialis, stationed the IXth legion. As so often in the history of Rome, where a legion went, there went Rome; tourists can still see the massive wall of York, initially built by the Romans, the roads which lead from the city still form an essential part of the transport net, while the very name given to it 'Eburacum' is the name from which the Scandinavian name for the city 'Jorvik' and thus the modern name, York is derived.

Throughout the history of the Roman Empire, the city of York would play an important part. It would be the supply base from which the famous Roman Governor, Gnaeus Julius Agricola, would launch his attacks on the Caledonians tribes to the north; the great emperor Hadrian most likely visited the city on the way north to build that famous wall. It was most likely under his reign (117-138 AD), that the city became the headquarters of the VIth legion, its unfortunate predecessor having been sent out to the east some years previously to guard the Euphrates frontier of the empire, and, according to some, was wiped out fighting the Persians and Jews during the revolt of Simon Bar Kochba.

The peace which Hadrian and his immediate predecessors and successors created, did not last; by 192 AD, with the murder of the deranged emperor Commodus, the governors of the armies of Britain, the lower Danube and the Euphrates region, attempted to seize the imperial purple. Five years of ferocious civil war ended, when the most able of them, the grim Septimius Severus, killed both of his rivals, and became the unquestioned leader of the Roman state.

Once again the city and environs of York, became the backdrop of a Roman emperor on campaign, as the ruthless and indomitable Severus, tried to pacify the north of the island of Britain. Marching, as so many English kings would later do, with decidedly mixed success, Severus marched to modern-day Moray, ravaging the lands of the Caledonians as he did so. Retiring to York in 211 AD, he died, exhausted by his exertions. As so often in its history, the city was the scene of a death which would cause bloodshed and chaos. Septimius was reputed to have said to his sons, Caracalla and Geta, 'Stick together, pay the army and ignore everything else.'

This proved to be a fairly concise piece of advice from a dying dictator, which alas, was not followed, as Caracalla had his brother murdered soon after.

The murder of Caracalla himself in 217 AD, was the signal for a series of ferocious civil wars in the Empire, together with a quite unparalleled number of barbarian invasions, from which the province of Britannia, oddly enough, was very rarely affected.

Towards the end of the second century, the great emperor Diocletian managed to bring the empire back into some sort of order, and once again, peace – of sorts – broke out in the Roman world. Towards the end of the century, however, Britannia itself was attacked from the sea by various peoples from the area of the River Rhine such as the Franks and the Saxons, the latter of whom, would soon seize the province for themselves and rule an Empire the like of which has never been seen.

The northern part of the province, now called Britannia Inferior, as a result of a reform of Caracalla, had its headquarters at York, which, again became the scene of a notable Roman death when one of the successors of Diocletian, Constantius Chlorus, died in 306 AD. Constantius had come to Britain to put down the revolt of Carausius, a swashbuckling individual, who had managed to make Britain independent of the Empire for a long period at the end of the third century.

Constantius had before he died, conducted a campaign against the Caledonian tribes to the north, and had carried out some much-needed reconstruction of the walls and docks of York. On his death, his murderous and unpleasant son, Constantine, was hailed as Emperor. Constantine would display considerable talents in the near future, chief of which was his remarkable ability to kill any opponents who crossed his path, and the emphasis he placed on being a sort of divine saviour who alone could restore the Roman Empire to its old glory. On his death in 337 AD, he had managed to kill any opponent within reach (including his own son) place a huge burden of taxes on the Roman people, and had introduced Christianity as the state religion. For these highly questionable reasons, later historians have given him the totally undeserved title of 'The Great'.

With the death of Constantine, the civil wars of the previous century would be replicated in the wars of Constantine's sons, of whom Constantius II would be the eventual winner.

The island of Britannia, would suffer considerably from the chaos of the mid 4th century, as increasing numbers of

Roman Emperor Constantine 'The Great' who used apostate Christianity to further his own ends. His statue sits in front of York Minster.

Picts, Saxons and Irish would attack and ravage the island. These attacks would culminate in a huge raid in 367 AD, when a concerted attack by all three peoples, would overrun the entire province. The emperor Valentinian I, beset by attacks by the Goths and Franks, was unable to come to the assistance of Britannia himself, so sent one of his best generals, Theodosius to restore order. This great general managed to expel the raiders from a province which had been thoroughly ravaged by the time he had completed his task.

The island province would be the centre again of a hiatus in the Roman world, when in 383 AD, a soldier in Britain named Magnus Maximus declared himself emperor and marched on Rome. Magnus must have been a man of considerable stature, as he managed to overrun the Western part of the empire before being captured and put to death in 388 AD. He had married a Celtic princess, Elen, and his name is still remembered in Celtic folklore as Macsen Wledig, the battle standard he carried on campaign, a dragon on a purple background, is claimed by Welsh historians as the origin of the red dragon flag of Wales.

The repeated raids, together with the civil wars at the end of the fourth century, seem to have had little effect on the whole of Roman Britain. However, with the inept Emperor Honorius now on the throne of the Western Roman Empire, things soon changed. Beset on the Danubian frontier by the raids of Alaric the Goth, the regent of the West, Stilicho, was forced to strip Britannia of some of its troops; by 405 AD, with the invasion of Italy by King Radagaisus, no help could be sent to Britain by the Imperial Government.

In the last days of 405 AD, thanks to the majority of imperial troops fighting in Italy, a huge band of Barbarians, Seuves, Vandals, Alans and Burgundians, aided by the fact that the River Rhine had frozen from bank to bank, swept over the River and overran Gaul.

The Roman Empire was in decline and the weak ruler of the Western part, Honorius, paid little heed to the problems of raider incursions in the provinces. Here he is seen feeding poultry, his favorite pastime, as secretaries charged with urgent affairs have to wait.

From this point, the Roman Empire in the West can be stated to have fallen. In Britain, cut off from the Imperial Government in Ravenna, consternation reigned. The army still extant in the province declared some of its officers emperors, killed them, and then followed a promoted ranker, Constantine III over the sea to try to regain the province of Gaul. After a few successes, Constantine was killed and the province of Gaul became a battleground for the various tribes which had invaded it.

In 410 AD, the position of the Britons, who, despite some doubts of later historians, had hardly any troops left to defend them from invasion, received the famous rescript of Honorius, telling them to look after themselves. Though this was merely a short-term suggestion by the central government telling the British provincials to help themselves against marauders, the very fact it was issued shows just how deplorable things had become. With the stripping of the army from Britannia, the overrunning of Gaul and Spain, the sacking of Rome in 410 AD by Alaric the Goth, the Roman province of Britain found itself on its own. But not for long.

The isolation of the province of Britannia, soon proved to be the signal for the barbarian tribes along the North Sea's eastern shore to launch raid after raid on the now almost defenceless province; the eastern geography of the island, with the great rivers of the Thames, Humber, Ouse, Tees and Tyne, proved to be excellent invasion routes for the sea-borne invaders which would soon make the old Roman province their own. From the mouths of the Rhine, from modern day Belgium and Holland, from Germany between the Weser and the Elbe, and from Jutland and Schleswig Holstein the raiders would come.

Along the river valleys of England, along its long coast, the eastern peoples soon landed. The native Celtic people, demoralised and dispirited, were rapidly overcome. Despite the campaigns of Ambrosius Aurelianus, a Romanised Britain, and the semi-mythical King Arthur, the Celts of Britain were rapidly overwhelmed. In just under two centuries, a group of disparate peoples from the eastern ocean, had managed to overwhelm a huge Roman province; this is a feat which is quite remarkable, since, unlike the Roman invasion of Britain, and the overrunning of the Rhine by the Barbarians, this conquest was not directed by one single leader, or a group of tribes working together. Some historians have stated that the numbers of Jutes, Saxons etc, who invaded Britain, were judging by the populations they conquered, were far larger than the invaders who later conquered Gaul and Spain. By the end of the 6th century, as anyone who has read the Anglo-Saxon Chronicles will be aware, most of Britain south of the Tees and east of the Severn was in the hands of the new peoples.

The very abundance of rivers and roads in Yorkshire made it easy meat for the invaders from the seas. Settling along the Humber, their land was initially called by the British, Deira, from the Celtic 'Water Dwellers'. By 590AD, the presence of the invaders had caused such distress amongst the native peoples of Britain, that the lord of Goddodin, an area round modern-day Edinburgh, launched a huge invasion of the Deirans' land, with the intention of taking from them the lately-lost city of Catraeth.

This invasion, immortalised by the poem 'Y Gododdin' by the poet Aneurin, managed to sweep down to Catraeth itself, only to be wiped out by a Deiran army. By then, however, the Saxon warriors were acquiring a fierce reputation for fighting on foot; after overwhelming their mounted opponents by sheer weight of numbers and superior iron weaponry.

The end of the sixth century saw the province of Britannia turned into the lands of the Anglo-Saxons: Wessex, East Anglia, Kent, Northumbria and Mercia. In 604AD, the king of Bernicia, a land round the river Tweed, had managed to unite his land with that of

With the decline of the Roman Empire the invasion of these shores by Jutes and Saxons became a regular event.

Deira, forming the lands of Northumbria to the North of the Humber River.

Despite the frequent wars between the now Anglo-Saxon kingdoms, by the end of the 8th century the kingdoms of England had roughly coalesced into the Kingdoms stated above. Christianity had been introduced into the lands of the English, and a spirited cultural renaissance had begun in the abbeys of Northumbria and Mercia. The gradual improvement of the climate had made the English Kingdoms like their continental counterparts, wealthy and fertile.

This was why the Vikings attacked them.

The Vikings is a collective noun given to the men from the modern-day Scandinavian countries, who from the late 8th century began to pillage and plunder Christendom.

What caused the Vikings (from the Norse nouns viking and vikingr, a pirate raid or pirate) to start their descent upon the West is as yet unclear; some authorities say it was because of the increasing power of the kings and nobles who were squeezing the small men and farmers off the land; others state it was due to the growing land hunger of a population, which, due to the better climatic conditions had increased to a degree which left the current amount of land unable to support them.

Whatever the reasons, soon the low-profiled ships, superb engines of travel, would soon be ravaging the whole of Western Christendom. In 793, the island of Lindsifarne off the Northumbrian coast had been ravaged. For the next few decades, the raids increased in number and savagery. For a few years, the Saxon lords were able to resist these descents of their Scandinavian cousins, however, in the words of the historian Sir Charles Oman 'by the mid 9th century, the whole of Scandinavian manhood seems to have taken to the oceans.' In 845 AD, Angleland, sailed up the Humber and occupied York. Two Northumbrian kings were killed in the battles that followed, and the ancient Kingdom of Northumbria began to become part of the Viking polity. Stopping on their way only to conquer part of Mercia, the Viking hordes, mounted on horses, singing the praises of Odin and Thor (though not alas, wearing horned helmets, which appear to have been a much later invention by romantic Victorian writers,) swept into, and occupied, East Anglia.

It was the turn of Wessex next; a Viking army under the command of a leader called Guthrum, swept into the kingdom of the West Saxons. By 878, most of the land of Wessex was occupied, but at this point, perhaps the greatest Englishman who has ever lived entered the scene: Alfred of Wessex.

Hurriedly raised as king by a remnant of the West Saxon polity, Alfred fought doggedly to free Wessex from the invaders. Owing to his skill, the wish of many of the Viking warriors to settle down and become farmers and the fact that the first great wave of Viking invasions was over, Alfred managed to drive out the invaders and free England roughly from a line running south-east from Liverpool to London.

By reforming mobilisation procedures of Wessex, building fortified towns and creating a new navy, Alfred managed to increase the power and prosperity of the land which he had so ably defended. In 899 he died, leaving to his successor Edward the Elder, a mighty military machine, and a lesson to succeeding generations on how a person can rule and reform and still be called 'the Great'.

Under Alfred's militaristic son, the West-Saxon conquest continued. In 910, Edward shattered an invasion of Mercia at Tettenhall in Staffordshire, and by following a policy of advancing into an area and building a fortress to dominate it (much like a later Edward in Wales at the end of the 13th century) Edward the Elder managed to advance the Saxon frontier to a line drawn from Liverpool-Manchester-Sheffield-Lincoln. (Experts in phonetics will

Easy pickings for the Viking invaders – a Christian monastry receives a visit from a raiding band of norsemen.

remark on the fact that the accent of the people living north of this line is still noticeably different to that south of it)

In 924, Edward died, and his son Athelstan came to the throne.

Perhaps the greatest of all the West Saxon kings, Athelstan, rapidly made his presence felt. He married one of his sisters to the Norse king of York, Sigtrygg. This worthy died a little later, and his successor, a born troublemaker called Olaf, promptly seized power in York. This did not sit well with the West-Saxon king, who promptly invaded Northumbria, sacked York and drove Olaf away.

Olaf tried to regain the Northumbrian throne with the help of his father-in-law, the lugubrious Constantine of the Scots. Thinking both of them needed a lesson to be learned, Athelstan led a huge invasion of the land of the Scotti, which ended with the army of the Saxons ravaging the land almost as far as Aberdeen, and the fleet which accompanied it sacking the northern kingdom as far as the Moray Firth.

This invasion appalled Constantine and the other petty kings of Britain, and the upshot was that Constantine and Olaf planned a massive counter-invasion.

The result was Brunanburh.

Alfred the Great.

BATTLEFIELD YORKSHIRE: A COUNTY AT WAR 937-1461

The Pennines hills to the west of the Wolds funnel the roads north-south into a natural invasion route. The Humber River gives easy access to the heart of Yorkshire making it the obvious choice for invaders from the sea.

NORTHALLERTON
1138 •

BYLAND
1322 •

BOROUGHBRIDGE •
1322

MYTON
1319 •

STAMFORDBRIDGE
• 1066

York ○

TOWTON •
1461

• GATE FULFORD
1066

WAKEFIELD •
1460

BRUNANBURH •
937

CHAPTER I

Brunanburh and the bloodbath at Sheffield 937 AD

'Never until now in this island, as books and scholars of old inform us, was there greater slaughter of an army with the sword's edge since the Angles and Saxons put ashore from the east'.

Such is the ringing declaration to be found in the Anglo-Saxon Chronicles under the year 937 AD.

Brunanburh was fought as the direct result of the growth in power of the Anglo-Saxon kingdom. From a few desperate men hiding in the forests of the south-west, the Saxon realm under Alfred, Edward the Elder and Athelstan had grown to incorporate all the land of mainland Britain south of the Mersey and Don. Under Athelstan's reign starting in 924 AD, an aggressive imperialistic mood seemed to beset the Saxon court, with campaigns being launched against many of its neighbours. The culmination of this was the terrible invasion launched in 934, which ravaged almost the whole of the land of the Scots from Edinburgh to Inverness.

This expansion not unnaturally appalled Constantine, the King of the Scots, while many of the other petty kings of the Northwest would have been thoroughly alarmed as well. The invasion of 934, could be the harbinger of outright annexation of the northern lands, an idea which, given the complete control of the south of mainland Britain the Saxon court now had, could not be described as a terrified flight of fancy.

What on earth could Constantine do? He could not attack Athelstan on his own; the only answer would be to forge an alliance of all the parties threatened by the Saxon expansion, and launch an invasion of the land of the Saxons himself.

Where was he to find these allies?

One was at hand immediately: his son-in-law, the Viking, Olaf of York, now residing in Dublin in Ireland, where he was in residence after having been driven from York by Athelstan in 927. The Vikings of Ireland had always displayed a taste for adventure, especially if plunder was the result. Constantine – and he was most likely the brains behind what happened next, would perhaps have sent ambassadors to Olaf to sound him out on attacking the Saxon realm. Olaf would probably have reacted with alacrity to the suggestion, and most likely visited Constantine in his kingdom.

With Olaf and the Vikings of Ireland with him, who else could Constantine persuade to assist him?

Next door to him, were the kingdoms of the Strathclyde Britons, in an area running roughly north from the Mersey to the Forth. They would have been thoroughly alarmed at the growth of English power, so would perhaps have agreed willingly to Constantine's suggestion.

Though on paper this was already an impressive alliance, something else had to be thrown in the pot to make it sizzle.

The fact that Constantine was planning an assault on the wealthy kingdom of the Saxons, would soon have become common knowledge amongst the fellow Vikings of Olaf. This news would have been disseminated along the trade routes to Scandinavia, where at the that time, there would have been a plethora of young warriors eager to gain land and glory. With the defeat of the Viking armies in England, together with the gradual growth of the Duchy of Normandy, which absorbed many restless northern spirits and the catastrophic defeat on the River Dyle in Belgium in 891 AD, which evicted the northmen from their base in Flanders, opportunities for expansion were a little limited by the end of the fourth decade of the 10th century.

Capitalising on this land hunger, Olaf and Constantine would have sent messengers to inform Olafís northern brethren as to the great invasion, which would soon take place.

It must be pointed out, that the invasion which followed can only be described as staggering in scope and complexity; a combination of Scots, Irish Vikings, British and Scots would have to be mobilised and concentrated from an area divided by two seas. They had to land in and march to, a place where all the armies could concentrate and fight. This invasion would be the 10th century equivalent of the D-Day landings. Taking into account the fact that the assault would take place only three years after Athelstan had ravaged Constantine's kingdom, we can only conclude that the preparations for the attack would have started almost straight after Athelstan had left Scotland in 934.

Where would Constantine be able to mobilise all these men in one place? Where would the coming battle be fought? The answer is given in the pages of several mediaeval chroniclers such as William of Malmesbury, John of Worcester, Roger of Hoveden and Florence of

Worcester. They all mention that in 937 AD a great fleet of ships under the command of Olaf entered the Humber.

We have found how Constantine managed to square the circle. It is this author's opinion that Constantine and Olaf agreed to launch both a sea and land invasion of England; Olaf, with the Vikings of Ireland, would sail to a point on the East Coast of mainland Britain and combine with the men of Scandinavia. Constantine, with the Scottish and British host, would advance south into Northumbria, and join with the sea host somewhere in Yorkshire, after the Viking armada sailed up the Humber.

This plan actually came to fruition, and this author must lavish praise on the co-commanders for their skill and foresight in managing to combine their forces so close to the English frontier.

What of the numbers of the invading force?

The chroniclers state that 615 ships sailed up the Humber to invade England. As the great Viking invasion of 1066 numbered only 300 ships, we can ignore this figure as being an example of mediaeval wishful thinking. However, as we are talking of practically the whole levy of Scotland, warriors from Strathclyde and Ireland, together with an untold number of men from Scandinavia, we can only state that the army coming to fight the English was huge. It must have easily outnumbered the armies which William of Normandy and Harald of Norway took to England in 1066. A figure of about 17-18,000 men would be accurate in this author's opinion.

Meanwhile, what of Athelstan?

Given the scale of the undertaking, he would have realised very quickly he was going to be attacked. He probably knew that Constantine would attack him, together with the other northern kings. Further, he would deduce that the invasion would likely come from the north.

Where in the north? We are told in the Chronicles of William of Malmesbury, that Athelstan 'awaited the invasion in his own land.' As the frontier of England at this time, ran along the Don and the Mersey, this author believes, following the idea of the military historian A.H.Burne, that Athelstan could have mustered the English force at Derby, to await an attack on either side of the Pennines. When the news came to him of the invasion along the East Coast, he would have marched

Athelstan's ring.

north to oppose the confederate armies. His army must have been somewhat the same size as that of his opponents, so over 30,000 men were gathered to do battle with each other.

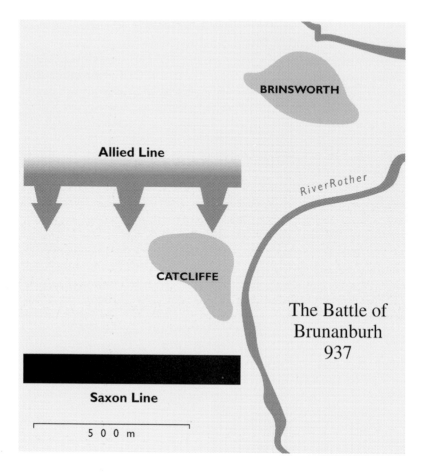

We are told that the battle was fought in Athelstan's own land, east of the Pennines, and taking into account that it was most unlikely that a Viking army, after disembarkation, would have allowed an enemy force to get between it and its ships, the battle must have been fought south of the Humber. As the old Roman roads led south from that region, over the Don (the old English frontier) the place which this author considers the battle was fought was between Sheffield and Rotherham, between Brinsworth and Catcliffe on the line of the old Roman Road.

As Athelstan had the benefit of local knowledge, he would probably have drawn up the English army in a defensive position on a piece of high land. All he had to do was wait for the invading army to attack him, since if the two armies merely 'observed' each other,

The supposed site of the battlefield of Brunanburh, between Rotherham and Sheffield.

each would be forced to leave when they had eaten the area bare. The invading army would have dissolved and all Olaf's and Constantine's efforts would have been in vain; they had to attack.

We are told very little about the battle; (Egil's saga, a 12th century description of the battle is riddled with inconsistencies) What we can deduce, was that it was an all-day battle with very little in the way of tactics being able to be displayed by any commander. As occurred in the wars of the Roses the two sides would have approached each other, attacked and fought.

The Anglo Saxon Chronicle tells us that the battle raged from sun up to sundown. It also says, (and if the duration of the battle if true, is probably not exaggerating) that the slaughter was on a scale not seen since the Anglo-Saxons first came to this land. The sheer scale of the casualties seems to bear this out; five kings and seven earls, together with a son of Constantine died. The Anglo-Saxon army itself was badly hit, at least one bishop and two of Athelstan's own cousins being among the fallen.

How did Athelstan win, why did so many of the enemies' leaders die?

It is this author's personal opinion that the answer lies in just one word: armour. At least one third of the confederate host, the Scots, together with many of the British, would have had little in the way of personal armour. When they charged the enemy (and common sense tells us they must have attacked), many of them would have been laid low by the hail of missiles that the Saxons would have discharged at them. When it came to close quarter fighting, the lack of armour must have been a terrible disadvantage to the confederate army.

It is this author's opinion, that the Scottish, who would have suffered terrible casualties anyway in the initial attack, would have been slaughtered, in close-quarter warfare. As the leaders at that innocent time were expected to lead from the front, this is the reason why five of the kings and Constantine's son died. If the Scottish broke, it is logical to assume that a flank of the Viking army would have become exposed (assuming the two forces fought next to each other.) the Saxon army would have swept round it, and the Viking force would have been overwhelmed.

Brunanburh was a victory the Anglo-Saxon realm would not see again till 1066. If Athelstan had lost the battle, the whole of England north of the Don, and probably north of the Wash would have become an independent kingdom. The Anglo-Saxon laws, culture and civilisation, would most likely not have been able to spring forth and fertilise and ennoble the world. From Brunanburh the origins of the English language, the common law of England and the British Empire would spring.

A coin dating from Athelstan's reign 925-939.

CHAPTER II

𝔜orkshire from 937 to 1066𝔄𝔇 – relative peace

The battle of Brunanburh, surprisingly, did not, at first, appear to have solved the problem of the Norse element in Northumbria. Athelstan the Magnificent, victor of Brunanburh, died in 939 AD. His brother, the Atheling (royal Prince) Edmund the deed-doer, succeeded him, and very soon afterwards, the egregious Olaf, with another pack of Vikings, appeared in York. With more courage than caution, the Northumbrians accepted him as their king; King Edmund, furious, came north to drive away Olaf, but in 940, as a result of the cunning of Wulfstan, Archbishop of York, who was to be a thorn in the flesh of Saxon kings for decades, a deal was brokered, which in effect made Northumbria independent again.

The Northumbrians were soon to rue their decision. Instead of realising that a period of peace and prosperity was required, Olaf immediately launched a campaign to add England north of the Tees to his domain. This was not to the liking of Edmund of the Saxons, who, from 942-944, launched three separate attacks on Northumbria.

The long-suffering Northumbrians seeing the writing on the wall, expelled Olaf and invited Edmund to be their lord and father. Once again, peace was to reign in Northumbria, however, the Viking ability to cause chaos whenever they so desired, was to show its face again, with one of the most notable warriors and psychopaths in the history of the 10th century: Eric Bloodaxe, the son of the great Norwegian King, Harald Fairhair.

In the year 946 a robber murdered King Edmund in his own villa at Pucklechurch. His brother Eadred succeeded to the throne. Probably urged on by that inveterate schemer, Archbishop Wulfstan, Eric invaded the land of Northumbria. The Northumbrians, by now thoroughly cowed by invaders coming into their land, accepted Eric as their king. Edred, enraged at this further display of perfidy, invaded Northumbria, sacked the Ripon, and was so feared by the Northumbrians that Eric was evicted from Northumbria with more

A reconstruction of a Viking longship. These vessels were regular visitors to the east coast and they found the rivers a useful means of reaching areas of Yorkshire to plunder.

haste than honour. By 954, Northumbria had to a large extent, become part of the Saxon realm. One of the reasons, being that Edred had managed to get his hands on Archbishop Wulfstan, and kept him under house arrest till he died, lamented by no-one, in 956.

The annexation of the kingdom of Northumbria by the Saxon kings marks the end of the second stage of the military history of Yorkshire. The following decades were, by the standards of the time, astoundingly peaceful. The Viking scourge appeared to have been met, the Saxons and the Norse of North-umbria lived in peace with one another, under a series of strong kings in Winchester, the Saxon capital.

This happy situation would last for about forty years, when once again the Norsemen would renew their invasions.

The catalyst of this new set of invasions, was Svein Forkbeard, King of Denmark. Unlike the earlier Viking attacks on England, which were in effect raids which became larger and larger, the next attacks would be directed by King Svein himself.

Why Svein should have decided to attack England is unclear; some historians say that a new generation of warriors was now coming to manhood and needed lands to attack and settle in; others say that once again the Norse kingdoms were overcrowded; others state that Svein wished that England be annexed so it could form part of a united trading empire. Whatever the reasons, the Danish invasions towards the end of the century, were on a scale not seen since the dark days of Alfred the Great.

Svein would be very lucky in that for most of the time, the most feckless monarch in the history of Saxon England, Ethelred the Unready, would rule England. (The ridiculous nickname is a pun on Ethelred's name; Ethelred is a compound word meaning 'noble-counsel' the nickname 'no-counsel' shows that Ethelred did not live up to his name or position, and had no advice to give his people during the dark days ahead.)

For over thirty years, the new Viking raiders, towards the end directed by Svein, would ravage and plunder England to a degree which would not be seen till the Norman conquest. Ethelred managed to keep his throne and his head by the simple procedure of executing, blinding or banishing any member of his kingdom who appeared to be a threat, and – to the rage of his people at the time and to the disgust of nationalistic historians through the ages, paying off the invaders with an ever larger degree of tribute.

The north of England with its strong Norse element suffered very little in this organised plunder. By 1013, when Svein sailed up the Humber and Trent to Gainsborough, the northern people acknowledged Svein as their king. By 1014, when Svein died, and his son Canute of Denmark succeeded him, almost the whole of England had accepted the Danes as their masters. In 1016, Ethelred himself died and, despite all that Edmund of the Ironside, the heroic son of Ethelred could do, on Edmund's death in 1016, there was no scion of the West-Saxon house to take up the sword against Canute. In 1017, in the expressive words of the Anglo-Saxon chronicles

Edmund Ironside meets Canute for the first time.

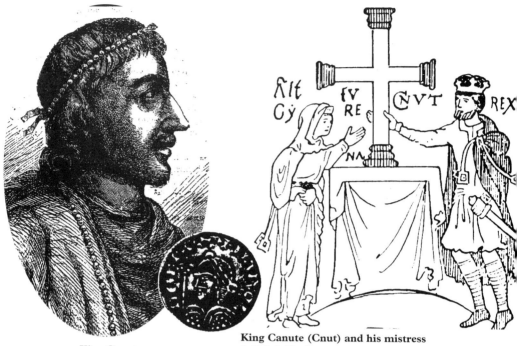

King Canute

King Canute (Cnut) and his mistress (wife) Aelfgyfu.

'Canute received the entire kingdom'.

Canute reigned from 1016 to 1035. To the astonishment of contemporaries and later generations of historians, apart from a few assassinations and banishings, his rule, in England at any rate – he also ruled a large part of Scandinavia – was not only peaceful but also just.

Very little is known of any military activity in Yorkshire during Canute's reign. The Earl of Northumbria, Siward, ruled it quite well. The only known outburst of campaigning occurred when Siward led an army to ravage Scotland in 1054.

Siward died in 1055. This would be the date from which many of the troubles which would later afflict the English realm would spring.

On the death of Canute, England had almost been yanked into civil war as a result of two of Canute's son claiming the throne: Harald Harefoot, the son of Canute and his English mistress, Aelfgyfu, and Harthacnut, Canute's son by Ethelred's widow, Emma of Normandy. The death of both of these singularly unprepossessing men, left the English without a king. One however, was literally waiting in the wings: Edward, the son of Ethelred, who had taken refuge in Normandy after Ethelred had fled England before the invasions of Svein.

The death of his rivals, meant that Edward – unquestionably descended from the line of old Saxon kings – was the only real candidate for the kingship, which is why he entered England unopposed in 1042, and was crowned the following year.

As Edward, by his reign and his death would affect the history not only of Yorkshire, but of England, it is necessary to examine carefully what he did as king and why.

Since his father's death, Edward had spent almost all his life at the Norman court. Contrary to many historians' beliefs, he had not been very well treated there. In 1036, following the death of Canute, he and his elder brother, Alfred, had tried to enter England to seize the throne. Alfred had been captured by Earl Godwin of Wessex, who – most likely given an ungentle hint by Harald, had handed him over to Harald, who immediately executed Alfred's attendants, and then blinded Alfred so viciously, that he died a few days later.

Edward – a born survivor – returned to Normandy, with his life and sight intact. When he became king of England in 1042, it cannot be said that he had had a very happy life. One of the English Earl's who greeted him, Godwin, he personally hated. Owing to the hiatus following the death of Canute and his own crowning, a lot of the king's power had evaporated, and to the end of his life, he was to be something of a figurehead. This previous experience, coupled with the knowledge that he had become king because there was no one else around, along with the fact that he had been compelled to marry Godwin's daughter as part of an agreement in order to become king, would have made a much stronger character than Edward a pretty suspicious monarch.

Edward, according to recent historians, had a habit of listening to the man who had shouted last and loudest at him. His policy (if it can be called one) veered from one idea to the next, and the fact that he managed to die peacefully, in bed, which his next three successors did not do, owed more to the fact that his other rivals in Normandy, England or Scandinavia, died before he did.

Throughout his reign, the House of Godwin, the leader of which, following the death of Godwin himself in 1053, would be the unfortunate Harold, would dominate him. It was probably at Harold's instigation, that Edward would make the most catastrophic decision of his career: the naming of Tostig as Earl of Northumbria in 1055.

When Siward died his only heir was an infant boy, Waltheof. It was essential that a man who had the ability to contain this turbulent land hold the north; Harold suggested that the earldom be given to his brother, Tostig.

As Harold was the strong man in England at this time, Edward, who, despite his saintly (and totally undeserved) reputation, was a weak and feeble character, gave in to his battlelord's advice; Tostig was also, it appears, a favourite of Edward's.

Tostig was duly made Earl of Northumbria and sent north to govern from York, to the fury of the Northmen, who would have preferred a member of the house of Siward to a West Saxon.

Their dismay at getting a 'foreigner' as a lord was increased as soon as Tostig took over the lordship of the north. Always a violent place, where the blood feud was a legal right, the area had it seems, completely fallen into a state of near-anarchy as Siward slipped in to the grave. Tostig set about his task by ruling with an iron hand. Taxes were collected with zeal and efficiency, robbers hung without mercy and the blood feud abolished. If the men of the north did not appear to see the logic of Tostig's acts, he persuaded them by quite simply arranging for murder squads to eleminate the more vehement of his critics.

The enforced peace, though helpful to commerce, did not do much to add to Tostig's popularity. The atmosphere began to resemble that of a pressure cooker. In 1065, while Tostig was on a visit to the south, the north burst into revolt; Tostig's own men were slaughtered, and the men of the north went on a rampage advancing to the south and sacking many towns. The leaders of the revolt claimed no disloyalty to Edward, but insisted that Tostig should be removed as Earl. At a Royal Council held to discuss the event, Harold, seeing the north would not submit to his brother any longer, advised Edward to submit to the rebels' demands. Morcar, the son of Leofric of Mercia was elected earl. Tostig, in a rage, departed from the court vowing vengeance.

Edward died in January 1066, and Harold Godwinson, Earl of Wessex, was elected King of England unanimously by the Witan (the Anglo-Saxon Parliament) He would prove himself to be a brave, intelligent and, indeed, great and merciful man, but, as the Anglo-Saxon Chronicles state 'he had little peace during the time he ruled the kingdom'.

Though the great men of England had elected Harold, his election caused consternation in Normandy. The Duke of the Normans, the ruthless and able William the Bastard, had claimed the Kingdom of England his by right, owing to the fact that Edward had promised it

Harold swearing to maintain the right of the Duke of Normandy to the Throne of England.

to him years earlier, and that on a visit to Normandy in 1064, Harold had promised William that he would acknowledge William as king when Edward died.

It should be pointed out, that if Harold did visit Normandy, the oath taken to William was almost certainly one taken under duress; there is no evidence at all that Edward had promised the throne to William. The election of Harold as king therefore, was quite legal and – by the standards of the time – totally constitutional.

Despite the validity of his election, Harold would be faced by not one, but two enemies, since not only would William make an attempt at invasion, but also so would another, even more ruthless individual: Harald Hardrada, ('the bad') King of Norway.

Harald of Norway, after a lifetime of adventure, massacres and murder, had become joint-king of Norway in 1046. Following the death of his nephew, Magnus, the following year, he became sole king of Norway.

A totally amoral man, Harald killed any who opposed him, ravaged the land of Denmark, sacked the town of Hedeby, and by 1066, had managed to place over the land of Norway what can only be described as a military dictatorship.

William at least had some legal justification to invade England. Harald it seems, had an empty treasury and a visit from Tostig, who had gone into exile in order to seek a foreign lord to help him regain his lands, pointed out the obvious: if he invaded England, Tostig would help him gain the throne and England's gold, while Tostig would in return, get Northumbria back. Harald of Norway needed no other persuading; without a shred of legal right, with the cheerful shamelessness characteristic of the Vikings, Harald announced he would invade England.

CHAPTER III

Gate Fulford and Stamfordbridge 1066

From the beginning of his reign, Harold of England would be faced with a situation never faced by this land before or since; two different invasions would be launched from two different directions almost at the same time. Not even in the dark days of the Second World War would this country be faced with such a predicament. It is not to the discredit of Harold that he failed to overcome the difficulties; we can only be amazed he came so close to success.

Harold, realising he would be facing Duke William in battle, took station with many of his troops on the south coast. He felt that the north, now in the hands of Morcar and his brother Edwin, earl of Mercia, would be able to hold its own. It appears at this time that Harold, together with the rest of the English establishment, either did not know, or did not take seriously, the threat from Norway. This situation appeared to be substantiated, when the treacherous Tostig, with mercenaries hired in Flanders, launched a series of raids on the English mainland. Edwin and Morcar soundly repulsed him when he tried to land in Lincolnshire, due mostly to the fact his men deserted him at the first opportunity. Tostig proceeded to sail north to Scotland, to await the fleet of Harald of Norway.

Harald of Norway had been busily preparing for the invasion of England ever since the visit by Tostig. Taking into account the fact that the invasion was so huge, and that a great deal of trade occurred between Norway and England, it is incredible that no wind of the preparations reached Harold of England.

By all accounts, the fleet that left Sogne Fjord was a huge one, of well over 200 ships. King Harald's army, according to some sources, would have been well over 12,000 strong. This was an army which had been hardened by over twenty years continuous fighting, and consisted of veterans of battles as far afield as Russia and Byzantium. As Harald had called a half levy of the men in his kingdom (a mobilisation order) he took with him the cream of the fighting men of Norway. Almost all would be possessed of armour, helmet, shield and weapons, a fact, which would be of consequence a few days later, in a manner which many historians have unaccountably ignored.

Harald set sail at the end of August. The historian, Snorri Sturlson writing over a century later, states that not only some of his men, but Harald himself was afflicted by dreams, telling him that he and his army would soon be food for the wolves. Harald appears to have taken some very strange precautions in leaving Norway; he left one of his sons behind as regent for the lands, and took one of his wives and two of his daughters with him on the voyage.

Harald sailed to the Shetland and Orkney Islands, where he was joined by allies from these regions. Pausing only to ravage the coasts of Scotland, the Norwegian fleet swept south, sacked Scarborough, and then entered the Humber, where Tostig was waiting for them.

The Battle of Gate Fulford

The contemporary reports state that this invasion came as a complete shock to Edwin and Morcar, not to mention Harold. It is believed that as Harald raided the area of Cleveland on about the 8th of September. He sailed down the East Coast and up the Humber, reaching the source of the Humber about the 18th. If this is true, it appears that Earl Morcar and Earl Edwin, had very little time to mobilise their forces to meet Hardrada. This goes a good way in explaining what happened next.

Hardrada beached his ships at Ricall, on the east bank of the Ouse, about nine miles from York. Leaving a force to guard his ships, he led his army, under his famous standard 'Land Ravager' to York.

On the 20th September Earls Edwin and Morcar, with the forces they had mobilised, would have looked out from the walls of York, to see the Viking host, about 9,000 strong. Taking into account the fact they would not have been able to mobilise the hosts of Northumbria and Mercia, only some local levies, together with their own households, we cannot believe they would have commanded a force of more than 6,000.

In this situation, the most prudent decision would perhaps have been to man the walls of York, and await the arrival of King Harold, to whom they must have sent messengers as soon as they had heard of the approaching Norwegian Armada. Instead, the two earls (who neither here nor later would display much intelligence or even basic common sense) elected to march out and fight the Viking host.

It must be pointed out that not only were the troops of Morcar and Edwin probably outnumbered by Hardrada's men, but they were almost certainly more inexperienced and poorly armed and armoured. These facts would become all too apparent when the two armies met.

The two armies drew up in line, at Gate Fulford, a little to the south of York; the west wing of each host rested on the Ouse, the east wing on a ditch which ran north to south, conveniently delineating the area.

The battle of Gate Fulford is easily told: the two armies advanced, and like a battle in the wars of the Roses, clashed together. The fight was of very short duration; the numbers of the Norwegian army, their greater experience, the quality of the armour and the individual skills of the Viking host enabled the Norwegian army in a very short

Harold receives news of the invasion.

time to smash the English army to smithereens. The extremely unreliable chronicler, Snorri Sturlson, mentions the fact that many of the English died by drowning in trying to cross the ditch and river to escape the Norwegians.

At the cost of minimal casualties (in this author's opinion) Hardrada and Tostig must have killed at least 3,000 of the English army, and were now in a position to overrun the earldom of Northumbria. It should be pointed out that both Edwin and Morcar escaped from the battle. Given what happened to the losing side at Stamfordbridge and Hastings a little later, when almost all the leaders of these armies were killed, this conspicuous survival seems to be a little strange. Either the two earls did not take part in the battle, or they made their escape from the combat rather precipitately, which would explain perhaps the rather one-sided nature of the battle.

With the army of the north shattered a short distance from their town, the authorities of York sent ambassadors to Hardrada and Tostig to sue for terms. Many historians have stated that this action shows the feeling of northern separatism, which was supposed to be rampant at this time in the north. To this author, it merely smacks of a healthy degree of common sense on the part of the York fathers.

Hardrada – showing a surprising degree of mercy given his past dubious record – agreed that his men would not enter York, but would take provisions from the city, and hostages who would join with him and Tostig, on their march south to conquer the rest of England.

It was agreed that the handover of hostages would take place at Stamfordbridge, a bridge over the River Derwent about eight miles east of York. At this time, Stamfordbridge was the junction of several roads in Yorkshire, and was therefore, a good place to gather provisions and supplies without entering York.

The date given for the handover, was 24th September. On the morning of that day, Hardrada left the Viking fleet at Ricall, and marched to Stamfordbridge.

The Battle of Stamfordbridge 1066

The rather unreliable historian, Snorri Sturlson, states that when Hardrada marched to Stamfordbridge, he took with him only two-thirds of his army. Given the rather one-sided battle of Gate Fulford, this would mean the army which he took with him was strictly for the gathering of provisions, and we would suggest that it would be less than 7,000-8,000 men. Sturlson also states that Hardrada allowed his men to come lightly armed to the meeting place, thinking (and why shouldn't he?) that he would face no opposition at all in the taking of hostages. He also states, the army marched in what can only be called a holiday atmosphere. Given the totality of the victory they had won on the 20th, this is only to be expected.

As the meeting place was over several miles from Riccal, and as first light was about 6 am at this time of the year, we can only assume that Hardrada after mustering and choosing his men got to Stamfordbridge some time after midday. It seems that the entire army was in a confident and casual mood, with no thought given to the fact that they could be in danger.

But they had underestimated King Harold of England.

Upon receiving news of the invasion of the north, King Harold realised he was in a strategically appalling predicament: if he stayed where he was on the south coast, Hardrada and Tostig would have the time to occupy the north and to establish themselves. They would then undoubtedly march south to try to overthrow him. If he did march north however, he would leave the coast wide open to Duke William's invasion from Normandy.

It is to his eternal credit that Harold, upon receiving news of the Norwegian invasion at the head of his dreaded housecarls regarded as being the best troops in Europe at that time and summoning the levies of the counties he rode through, elected to march north to York to meet the Viking threat. So swift was his march, that by the evening of 24th of September, at the head of about 8,000 men, Harold had reached Tadcaster, about ten miles south west of York. The following day, soon after daybreak, he marshalled his troops and marched to York.

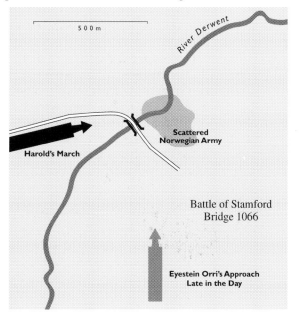

500 m

River Derwent

Scattered
Norwegian Army

Harold's March

Battle of Stamford
Bridge 1066

Eyestein Orri's Approach
Late in the Day

The speed of his advance was probably due to the fact that most of his men were mounted, and, in the Saxon way, only dismounted to fight. Whatever the reason, to the incredulity and delight of the City of York, Harold' s army (he had probably ridden ahead to get information) entered York at about mid-day on the 25th.

Having being appraised of the situation, and being informed that the Norwegian army would be placed at Stamfordbridge, Harold of England, with a touch of true genius, decided to march that very day and attack Hardrada.

At Stamfordbridge, Hardrada, who probably had only reached the spot some minutes before, was startled to see a large force of men approach on the York Road. To his consternation, he saw the strangers pass through the village of Gate Helmsley.

The English had arrived in force.

It is most likely that much of the Norwegian force was scattered in collecting supplies, and that most of them were on the west bank of the river Derwent. Hardrada had no other option than to send a message to the men at Ricall frantically ordering them to march to his aid, get his men together and pull his men across the bridge to take position on the east bank.

The consternation of the Norwegian host can only be imagined, and though the messengers despatched by Hardrada got through to Ricall, it is clear that the Norwegian host had been completely surprised by the bold tactics of King Harold.

Snori Sturlson, and other later historians state that before the battle, Harold went to the Norwegian host, and offered his brother a third of England if he would come back to his allegiance. When asked what Harold of England would give Harald of Norway, the heroic reply was, purportedly 'six good feet of English earth for a grave', or in Harald's case, seven feet as he was taller than most men.

This legend, alas, is not true; Harold would not have spent time offering a deal while he was advancing and with the Norwegian army so obviously in disarray, and it is hardly likely that Tostig, surrounded by Norwegians, would have been allowed to talk to Harold.

What probably happened is that there was a frantic race for the bridge, with the Norwegian army most likely losing whatever cohesion it had in getting across. It is this author' s opinion, that a great deal of Norwegians were killed in trying to get across the river. There is another legend, which states that for a while a single warrior held the English at bay, striking down all who opposed him, and was only despatched when an English soldier managed to get into a boat, paddle under him, and killed him by thrusting up a spear through a hole in the bridge thus impaling him. This is also a legend. The part of the Anglo-Saxon Chronicle, which mentions this incident, is a

View towards Gate Helmsley, Stamfordbridge. Note the rise in the ground as indicated by the road; this would have made it difficult for Harald of Norway to see the Saxons approaching.

The modern bridge at Stamfordbridge from the west. The 11th Century bridge would have been far smaller and consequently easier to defend.

Harald Hardrada at Stamfordbridge.

East bank of the Derwent as seen from the bridge. It is on this ground that the Norwegian army would have been attacked by the Saxons.

much later addition to the manuscript, and it is noticeable that this incident is not mentioned in the story of Snori Sturlson.

With the Norwegian army in retreat and with many of his men most likely scattered in looking for supplies, Hardrada, would have spent the next several minutes in bringing his army into some sort of order. This would explain the fact that the Anglo-Saxon army was able to cross over the river and to organise itself before they attacked the Norwegian host without being attacked themselves.

The battle on the east bank of the river, must have been a savage hand-to-hand affair. However, as at both Gate Fulford and Brunanburh, the side with the least armour was at a terrible disadvantage. The Norwegian army, with many of its men searching for supplies, others scattering to the four winds, and with, let it be noted, a lot of its men slaughtered on the west bank, would most likely have been outnumbered quite considerably by the English host. In the fighting which followed, both Hardrada and Tostig were

The Anglo Saxon Chronicle showing the entry of the account of the Battle of
Stamfordbridge (arrowed). Insets: The dragon standard of Wessex, coin of
Harold Godwinson, the Black Raven banner of Harald Hardrada.

struck down, and the Norwegian host completely routed.

It must have been at this time that the Norwegians from the base at Ricall entered the fray. Given the fact that the messengers had had to go all the way to Ricall to warn them of what was happening at Stamfordbridge, and that the men had to arm themselves and march the ten miles to the area, most likely having to cross the River Derwent to the east bank, we can only assume that it was not until about 3 pm, that they entered the fighting. We are told that the majority of the men from Ricall, led by Eyestein Orri, Hardrada's son-in-law, were quite exhausted by the time they got there, and some of them had had to throw off their coats of mail to help them move faster, facts which seem easy to believe.

It is most likely that the men of Orri were unable to hit the English as one body, as many of them would have fallen by the wayside in the advance to the north. When they finally reached the English, who by now must have completely routed the first Norwegian army, they must have been all but engulfed by the English army, and most of them, including Orri, slaughtered.

The Anglo-Saxon Chronicles state that after the rout, many of the Norwegians fled to their ships, that the Saxon army followed them, and slaughtered them, burning some of the ships at Ricall.

If this is true, it means that the English army had marched from Tadcaster to York, York to Stamfordbridge, a journey of about sixteen miles, fought a battle, and then pursued what was left of the Viking host to Ricall, a round trip of about twenty-eight miles.

Detail of the ironwork on the 'Old Dane's Door at Stillingfleet Church, near Selby, with a representation of a Viking longboat. The feature is said to commemorate the Battle of Stamfordbridge.

Whatever the facts, we can only make the following assumptions: that the decision to march north and attack the Norwegian host as soon as he got to York, was a decision of great courage by Harold, who had won one of the three great battles to be won by an English king in Yorkshire; that the Norwegian host was totally surprised by the English army when the battle started; that the lack of body armour and the fact that the Viking host was unprepared for the combat and was most likely scattered at the start of the combat was of great importance, and finally that the slaughter that day must have been frightful. We are told that of the 300 ships which came into the Humber in September, only 24 were needed to take the Norwegian army back. Even if this is an exaggeration we can conclude that the battle of Stamfordbridge smashed the military might of Norway for a generation.

At the end of the day, Harold offered terms to the remnant of the Viking host. The son of Hardrada, Prince Olaf, who appears to have been left in command of the ships at Riccal that day, was allowed to leave the kingdom under condition that he swore an oath never to come back and invade the realm again. Olaf appears to have taken this oath with alacrity, and returned to Norway. He appears to have wisely refrained from any military activities while king, and was given the affectionate nickname of Olaf the Quiet by a people who appreciated the peace he gave the realm after the tumultuous reign of Hardrada.

Harold, the last of the Saxon rulers, had most worthily shown he was great king and, had he not had the terrible luck to be faced with two invasions within a month, which led to his tragic death and defeat at Hastings, he would, in this author's opinion have shown himself to be a capable and just king and England may well have been spared the horrors and terrors of the following decades.

Present-day memorial.

CHAPTER IV

Towards a quiet period in Yorkshire 1066-1138

The years following the battle of Stamfordbridge would prove to be the most horrendous in the history of Yorkshire. King Harold, foolishly, raced down to the south coast on hearing of the landing of Duke William of Normandy at Pevensey. With an army which was outnumbered and exhausted, he recklessly gave battle to the Norman lord, and died with his housecarls around him at Hastings on 14th October, 1066.

On his march to London, William gave the English a taste of what he was to give them for the rest of his reign: he ravaged the area south

After the Battle of Hastings the body of King Harold is discovered amongst the slain.

of the capital so thoroughly, that for years afterwards the lands over which he marched remained desolate.

Having got himself crowned he left for Normandy, leaving his army to plunder the land at will. In 1067, William returned and marched north, overrunning Northumbria and building a castle at York. The following year he gave the Earldom of Northumbria to Robert De Commines, who, having made himself hated by his actions, marched to Durham to build a castle there. He and his men were trapped in the house of Aethelwine, the bishop of Durham. At this news, the north flew into revolt and an army led by Edgar the Atheling, the only scion on the West Saxon house now in England, marched on York. Yorkshire greeted him enthusiastically, but William managed to race north with an army to drive away Edgar and sack York.

King William the Conqueror.

Deliverance appeared to come to the English when a Danish fleet swept up the Humber in 1069. Once again the Atheling Edgar and a disparate rebel army arose to greet the Danes who were seen as deliverers. The

Clifford's Tower, York, built by William the Conqueror.

combined army swept into York, took it and slew the garrison.

This incident was the precursor to the most appalling act of William's reign. Gathering another army, he bribed the Danes to leave the land, and then marched again on York, which was completely sacked. In order to ensure no more revolts could occur in Northumbria, he marched north, killing every single man and boy he found. The area of the land was so thoroughly ravaged that it was estimated the area between York and Durham was totally devastated and an entire generation destroyed. By 1086, York was still deserted and much of the land lay desolate.

The situation was in no way assuaged by the fact that the Kingdom of Scotland was now ruled by the ferocious and devious Malcolm Canmore. Taking advantage of the chaos which now afflicted Northumbria Malcolm repeatedly invaded the north, ravaging and sacking the land in a manner as bad as William. This led to a huge invasion of Scotland in 1072, in which William marched as far as the Tay and forced Malcolm to become his vassal. This agreement had no effect whatsoever, since in 1079, Malcolm was on the warpath again. Invading and ravaging as far as the Tyne, he took much booty and it is surprising to hear that William did not appear to retaliate. He did react when the ever-wild people in that area murdered Bishop Walcher in 1080. William proceeded to build a castle on the Tyne, an area that is now given the name, Newcastle on Tyne.

This incident would be, it appears, the last military exploit of William at this time. By the ravaging and plundering of the land, William had brought to Yorkshire, the peace and justice of the charnel house. When he died in Rouen, in 1087 having managed to rupture himself when sacking the city of Nantes as cruelly as he had sacked York, the people of the north, may have taken some gratification in the fact that he died in agony, and that, as he had grown so immensely fat, when his body was

William the Conqueror towards the end of his life became obese and died in agony caused by a rupture suffered during the sacking of the city of Nantes, France, 1087.

stuffed into the coffin, it burst asunder, and those in the church of St Gervaise where he was buried, were nearly asphyxiated by the smell.

William was succeeded by his second son, William Rufus (so called because of his red hair), who would prove himself to be a strong king, as well as greedy, grasping (and if the not altogether unbiased mediaeval chroniclers are to be believed) an unabashed sodomite and a pagan. Though the first few years of his reign were spent in quelling revolts, the necropolis that was the north remained quiet, until Malcolm of Scotland invaded Northumbria again in 1091. William Rufus raised an army to fight his obstreperous northern neighbour, but a reconciliation was affected in which William promised to give Malcolm much land and gold in return for peace.

The Scots returned to the own land, and Malcolm found out very rapidly that Rufus, who refused to fulfil his part of the deal, had swindled him. In 1093, he visited Rufus at Gloucester, who arrogantly refused to see him. Enraged, he left England and returned the same year at the head of an army. This raid was to be his last however, since the Scottish king, who had so often tricked the English, was himself tricked by Robert Morel, Earl of Northumbria. Morel managed to trap Malcolm with some of his men and kill him and his son, Edward. Morel would not have much time to enjoy this victory, however, as he joined in a revolt against William, was captured and led to his castle of Bamburgh. Threatened with blinding if the castle did not surrender, his wife opened the gates to Rufus' men, and Morel was thrown in prison at Windsor.

Apart from Rufus aiding Edgar, the son of Malcolm Canmore and Margaret, an Anglo-Saxon Princess, to seize the throne of Scotland in 1097, the north and Yorkshire were left in peace throughout the reign of this strange man. When he died in a hunting accident in the New Forest

King William II, son of the Conqueror and surnamed Rufus.

(probably arranged by his ruthless brother, Henry) in 1100, the stage

William Rufus was killed in a hunting 'accident' in the New Forest in 1100 – this was likely arranged by his brother, Henry.

was set for a period of peace the north had not seen since the days of Siward.

The reasons for this are not very hard to understand: Henry was far too busy establishing himself on the English throne and fighting his incompetent elder brother, Robert, in Normandy, to bother too much about Scotland; in Scotland itself, Edgar's younger brother, David, who had been brought up at the Norman court, ruled Scotland south of the Forth almost as an independent viceroy, before he became king in 1124.

David busied himself by bringing some order to his

King David of Scotland

turbulent realm, and to do this, he invited many Norman and French knights to his lands to serve him. From this time, the great Scottish families such as the Bruces, Cummings, Stewarts, Urquharts and Lindsays start their tempestuous histories as Scottish families. With their help, he rapidly brought order to his land, a curious amalgam of English, Celtic, French and Flemish speakers. These changes by David would be the cause of one of the most peculiar incidents in the very peculiar military history of Yorkshire.

A period of peace ensued during the reign of King David I of Scotland, but trouble was in the making.

CHAPTER V

Battle of the Standard (Northallerton) 1138

H enry I died in 1135, in Rouen, the result it was said, of eating an inordinate amount of lampreys. Both England and Normandy were thrown into confusion as Henry, despite leaving over ten illegitimate children, left no legitimate male child. The choice as to who would rule England would be between Henry's easy-going but foolish nephew Stephen, and Henry's daughter, the Dowager German Empress Matilda, who would show herself as time passed to be an unpleasant and extremely arrogant virago.

Owing to the fact that he was actually in Normandy at the time of his uncle's death, Stephen was on the spot to sail to England and get himself crowned king. Though he was to rule for nineteen years, his was not to be a happy reign, for, as the Anglo-Saxon chronicle relates 'in this king's time all was strife, evil and robbery'.

Almost immediately, barons in England and Normandy began to revolt thinking – rightly as it turned out – that Stephen lacked the ruthlessness and savagery of his three predecessors. For most of his reign, Stephen would be on campaign, trying to quell the revolts of his vassals.

Henry, grandson of William the Conqueror, had no legitimate heir and so when he died his nephew Stephen became king of England.

In 1138, while Stephen was busily quelling revolts in the south of England, (with a notable lack of success), the Empress' cousin, David, King of the Scots, invaded England with a huge army. The reason given, that he was invading the realm in order to assist his helpless niece who had been wrongfully deprived of her just rights, can be completely ignored, as Stephen had been given liege homage by all the great men of the land. The real reason of course was that David was acting as any 'noble, chivalrous and just' King would do in this situation; doing his damnedest to grab any piece of land from a weak neighbour and to hell with anything else.

King Stephen.

It is very likely that the army which accompanied the king of the Scots was the largest army which a Scottish king ever led. According to the mediaeval chroniclers, Aelred and John of Hexham, the Scottish host consisted of men from Lothian, Moray, Galloway, the Highlands and even included some Norwegian mercenaries. It appears that the whole host of the Scottish war machine was mobilised. Given this, together with the fact that David was also accompanied by some French and Norman knights whom he had brought with him when he had assumed the throne of Scotland, we can say that the size of the Scottish force must have been at least 15,000 men.

The arms of the various groups of the Scots force varied considerably, from the, mailshirts, shields, swords, lances, and war-horses of the continental knights to the levies from Lothian, most of them descendants of the Anglo-Saxons who had left England in disgust after 1066 and the Highlanders and men of Galloway, armed with little more than shields, darts and swords.

David invaded England by crossing the River Tweed and proceeded to ravage the lands of Northumberland and Durham. If we are to believe Richard of Hexham and Aelred, the invasion was accompanied by quite appalling cruelties on the parts of some of the Scottish host; the Gallowegians in particular were accused of slaying priests at the alter and children at their mother's breasts. The Scottish force ravaged its way down to the Yorkshire border, which it crossed in August 1138.

The invasion of the Scots caused the local barons of Yorkshire to call out the feudal levy of the shire. King Stephen, who was then fighting the Empress Matilda, could offer little in the way of succour, but ordered some of the lords of the Midlands to march to assist the Yorkshiremen.

An illustration of King David dating from the 14th Century.

Bernard de Balliol, (whose distant descendant, John Balliol, would play a far more important and much less successful role in Scottish politics a century later) and William of Albermarle led this force. Their troops joined the Yorkshire levy, led by the Sheriff of Yorkshire, Walter l' Espec, somewhere near York, and the combined force marched out of the City, about 20th August, after being blessed by the aged Archbishop of York, Thurstan.

The English army, which can be stated to have been at least 9,000 strong, and was probably several thousand larger, presented a much more homogenous force than their opponents. The elite force of the army, were the armoured knights which rode with it. We can assume, as the cost of equipment for a knight was not as prohibitive as it would be at the end of the century, that at least 1,000 of the total English army could be described as being 'Chivalry'. The rest of the force consisted of foot levies, of which a large number were archers. This author would conservatively assume that at least 2,000 men of the English army which fought at Northallerton, were bowmen.

The make up of the armies of both sides was quite remarkable. French speaking descendants of the Norman knights who had invaded England in 1066, led both sides. A very substantial part of the Scottish army was Lowland infantry, whose ancestors had left England in disgust after the conquest. The consequence was that the ensuing battle would be fought between men who were closely related to each other, while the other ingredient in the military pot, the Celtic speaking Gallawegians, hated both French and English. This particular ethnic problem would have catastrophic consequences.

Archbishop Thurstan of York

It is interesting to consider how these forces were actually armed with the bow. As very few of the armies on the English side which fought in 1066 actually had archers, how could at least one sixth of the force be armed with bows less than a hundred years later? There is no real evidence to show that the Norman kings had encouraged the use of the bow, and as the overwhelming majority of the archers must have been English

**Archbishop Thurstan of York rousing the crowds to face the invaders from
Scotland.**

yeomen, then we can safely assume that very few of their number were Normans who emigrated to the area after 1066.

The English host reached Northallerton, about thirty miles north of York. The Scottish army was to the north of the village, and the actual battle took place on 22nd August 1138.

The Chronicler Aelred tells us, that the English were drawn up in one deep line. According to Aelred, the whole of the force fought dismounted, the knights on foot with the shire levies. Behind them, apparently were some lightly-armed country folk. The archers we are told, were 'mixed' with the knights and levies. The whole force was on the low east-west ridge, which is to be found a little to the north of Northallerton. With the army was a strange chariot, on which were placed the banners of the local saints, Saint John of Beverley, St Peter of York and Saint Wilfred of Ripon, together with the ' Godfather' of Northern English saints, Cuthbert of Durham.

We have very little information as to whether the Scottish army actually marched to attack the English, or vice versa, but we have information considering a rather interesting little incident which shows very clearly the social tensions which resulted in the progressive feudalisation of Scotland.

Upon meeting the English force, and seeing how they were arrayed, King David adopted the following plan: his own knights would dismount with archers arrayed to their flanks; they would advance with the Lothian shire levies and Highlanders and Gallowegians behind them. As soon as the knights attacked the English and made a gap in the English front, the Gallowegians, Lothian men and Highlanders would charge in and shatter the English line.

This rational suggestion was not to the liking of the Gallowegians and Highlanders in the Scottish host. Malise, the Earl of Strathearn, one of the earldoms north of the Forth said angrily,

'Why trust so much my king, to the goodwill of the Frenchmen? None of them, for all his mail, will go so far to the front as I, who fight unarmoured in today's battle.'

Alan de Percy, one of the Norman 'new men' of Scotland responded angrily, saying, ' Those are big words, and for your life you could not make it good.'

A furious altercation began between the Gaelic section of the force, and the French newcomers. Though, as most of the French knights could not speak Gaelic or English, and most of the Gaels could not speak French, very little must have been understood by either side.

King David, in despair, acting more in the dictates of justice than that of common sense gave in to the demands of the Gaelic section of his array, and allowed them to take the vanguard.

The resulting formation of the Scottish was that the centre was held by the Gallowegians whilst to their right, Prince Henry, David's son, led a large contingent of mounted knights, about 200 strong. Behind and to the left of the vanguard and were the levies of the Lothian, behind Prince Henry, the levies of Strathclyde. Behind the Gallowegians, stood the men of Moray, and behind these, with a very small bodyguard, was David himself.

Before the battle one of the English lords, Robert de Bruce, the direct ancestor of a rather more famous Robert the Bruce, went up to David and tried to make peace. As he, like many men, held land in both Scotland and England, his allegiance was understandably divided. His appeals for peace were drowned out by the taunts of the young knights in David's entourage, and he left, disavowing his homage to the Scottish King.

On the morning of the 22nd August, 1138 therefore, the Scottish army, consisting of Gaels, English and French, faced the English army, of which most of its leaders spoke French and its foot soldiers spoke only English.

The battle was opened by the Gallowegians, with the ancient Scottish battle cry of 'Albany, Albany!' as they charged the English line.

This charge was met with a hail of arrows from the English archers, who felled their foes by the hundred. In Aelred's vivid metaphor, 'The Gallowegians dropped dead to the ground, their bodies more filled with arrows than a hedgehog with quills.'

According to some reports the Gallowegians managed to come to sword strokes with the English line, to others they did not come to within ten paces. Aelred states that the 'Gallowegians returned time after time to the charge, but the arrows hurt them sorely.'

If this is true, then it appears unlikely that the Scots were able to reach the English force, since if they did, they must have been repulsed, and this would have made it very difficult for them to return to the fray again. The shattering losses of the Gallowegians who, bereft of body armour, would have made easy targets for the English archers, made them recoil and flee from the battle. The fact that their leaders, Donald and Ulgerich both fell on the field would have led to the confusion.

The sight of the vanguard reeling back would have had a deleterious effect on the rest of the Scottish host, many of whom took

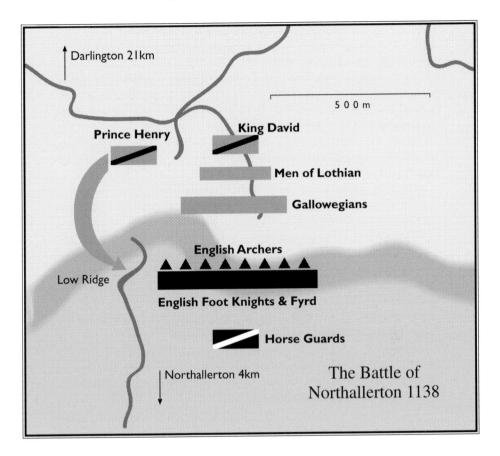

this opportunity to flee the field. The Scottish on the left, we are told, made only a feeble attempt to move forward and then promptly decamped.

Prince Henry, seeing the confusion and without orders from his father, launched an attack with his knights. This force managed to hew its way round the flanks of the English line, and get to the English encampment.

Unfortunately, after slaughtering some of the English grooms and varlets, Prince Henry realised that he was unsupported; the Strathclyde levies having decamped from the field as soon as they saw the Gallowegians in retreat. The Prince, seeing how things stood, ordered his men to throw away their badges and move back towards his own lines, mingling with the advance line of the English. He then gradually passed through the English line, and led his men at a moderate pace. He later managed to rejoin his father's army only after three days' riding from the English. Of the 200 knights he led into battle, we are told, only nineteen returned with him, a fact that seems to show how savage the fighting was when the Scottish knights breached the English line.

With his army visibly collapsing around him, King David ordered his highlanders to advance. With no desire to share the fate of the vanguard, this body of men also, elected to retreat. In despair, King David left the field with a small bodyguard of Norman and English knights.

So ended the battle of Northallerton.

If the chroniclers Richard and John of Hexham are to be believed, the battle lasted only a short while.

The numbers of the Scottish dead cannot be stated with any precision, but must have been at least 4,000, as any of those who were unable to walk away from the battle would most likely have been slaughtered on the spot by the English. The English losses must have been well under 1,000.

The reason for the defeat at Northallerton can be placed quite squarely on the shoulders of the reckless Gallowegians, whose lack of both restraint and body-armour made them easy meat for the English archers. The peculiar lack of attacking fervour shown by many contingents of the Scottish host can be explained perhaps by the unwillingness of the English of the Lothian to attack their fellow Saxons and the fact that there appeared to be a great degree of jealousy between the Gaelic factions in the Scottish host and the Foreign 'newcomers'. It would have to wait until the coming of the Bruce, when these differences would be subsumed in order to unite against the 'Auld enemy'.

A view of the battlefield as it stands today.

CHAPTER VI

Yorkshire, unscathed 1138-1319

The years of civil war under Stephen had remarkably little effect on Yorkshire, which flourished under Stephen's reign. Under his successor, Henry II surnamed 'Curtmantle', the first of the tempestuous line of the Plantagenet kings most of the fighting which occurred took place in France, where Henry would be soon involved in an interminable squabble against the French king. This situation would continue under Curtmantle's vicious and sadistic son, Richard the Lion Heart.

The only incident of interest occurred when the Scottish King, William the Lion (not so-called for his skill at arms, at which he was noticeably inept, but because of the Lion rampant coat-of-arms he wore) tried to get back from Richard the lands in Northumbria of which he had been deprived when he had managed to get himself captured by English knights near Alnwick.

Henry II.

When asked by William if he could have the lands returned to him, Richard, showing the mixture of arrogance and total lack of common sense which would stay with him through out his life, stated that William could keep the land if Richard could keep the castles! Given the fact that this was the 12th century, when the castle was supreme, it is not altogether surprising that William returned home in despair.

Richard's reign would be a long chapter

Henry II's son Richard I, the so-called Lion Heart, a bloodthirsty individual who would be taught some manners by Saladin.

of massacres and battles. However, most of these bloodbaths, would occur in the Holy Land, where he fought Saladin, or in Normandy and the Isle-de-France, where he would spend most of his life in a hammer-and-tongs war against the chilly Capetian King of France, the shrewd and cautious Philip Augustus.

Richard's death (for which he was entirely to blame) at an obscure castle in the Aquitaine, in 1199, meant that that most peculiar and deranged of English kings, John, Richard's brother, succeeded him.

Fortunately for Yorkshire, John would spend most of his reign fighting in France and Maine. Having lost almost all of Northern France however, John had to return to England with his tail between his legs, where his repeated demands for taxes, together with his rather questionable personal morals and habits, led to a full-scale revolt against his authority. He responded by ravaging the lands of his enemies and by embarking on a war ride through Yorkshire in the winter of 1215.

John's death in 1216 restored the peace, which was only intermittently broken over the next few years, when John's foolish and sybaritic son, Henry III, ruled England.

John I.

The only matter of real note which occurred in Yorkshire during this period, was the marriage in 1251, in York, of the Scottish king, Alexander III, to Henry's daughter, Margaret Plantagenet.

A huge amount of planning was necessary for such an event, which can be imagined when it is discovered that no fewer than 68,500 loaves would be required for the food for the wedding, together with 2,000 partridges and 1,000 chickens. At the wedding was the Lord Edward, the eldest son of Henry, who would have danced and feasted with the Scottish nobles with whom and whose descendants, he would,

King John's son, who became Henry III in 1216.

when king, have such a volatile relationship.

Edward succeeded to the English throne in 1272, and for the most part his relations with his northern neighbour were excellent. Alexander twice visited the English Court, and though both of Alexander's sons died before he did, Alexander managed to get the community of the realm to accept his daughter, Margaret of Norway, as heiress presumptive and there was no sign that Alexander's second wife (Margaret Plantaganet, had died in 1274), Yolande of Dreux would not be able to bear him more sons.

The marriage to Yolande, in 1285, was celebrated at Jedburgh Abbey, amidst the usual pomp and ceremony a royal wedding demanded. It appears however, that the marriage was doomed from the start, since at the wedding feast, apart from the minstrels, jugglers, thieves and prostitutes who usually attended such gatherings, there appeared a strange apparition more ghost than mortal at the end of a procession in the abbey. This weird being, disappeared as suddenly as it arrived, reducing the congregation to a state of stupefaction.

The more superstitious amongst the populace would not have been surprised to hear what happened next: in March 1286, Alexander, having attended a meeting of his council in Edinburgh, decided to visit his wife, now ensconced in the Royal manor of Kinghorn across the Firth of Forth, in the earldom of Fife.

His advisers begged him to reconsider, as the night was a wild one indeed. As Edinburgh was now one of the recognised royal dwellings of Scotland, we can only assume that Alexander was less concerned with having a warm bed for the night than indulging in his conjugal rights.

Alexander managed to cross the Forth unharmed, then rode along the clifftop on the south shore of the Earldom of Fife, and disappeared from the sight of his escort. His body was found on the sands below the cliffs with its neck broken; it is believed that his horse, scared by the wind, threw him to his death.

The nobles, commons and clergy of Scotland, immediately gathered and swore homage to Margaret, the maid of Norway, Alexander's granddaughter, as Sovereign of the Scots. These facts were passed on to Edward I, King of England, who despatched a ship to pick up the young heiress to take her to her new kingdom; when she died in the

Edward I.

Orkney Islands, on the way to Scotland, the consternation of the Scots can only be imagined.

The Scots, at a loss what to do, begged King Edward to adjudicate as to who should now be the new lord of Scotland. After a series of meetings with the representatives of the Scots, Edward scrupulously checked the claims of the men nearest in blood to the ancient house of Canmore: Robert Bruce of Carrick (whose ancestors had fought on both sides at the Battle of the Standard. and John Balliol (who ancestors had fought on only one side). As Balliol was unquestionably the nearest in blood to the dead Alexander, Edward decided he was the true king of the Scots, and duly pronounced himself to be king.

Unfortunately, Balliol was Edward's vassal for the lands he held in France and England. Edward proceeded to treat both Balliol and his kingdom therefore, as his subordinates, and in several humiliating incidents, forced him to appear before English courts to answer pleas against the Scottish crown.

The Scots very rapidly tired of this treatment, and forced their king (who throughout his life would get a very rough ride) to rebel against Edward. The only result of this was that in 1296, Edward invaded Scotland, sacked Berwick and routed the Scots at Dunbar.

Most of the Scottish nobility were taken prisoner here, together with their hapless king. Edward garrisoned the most important castles of Scotland, while Balliol – to his relief one thinks – was sent to one comfortable prison after another in England and France. Edward, thinking he now had Scottish affairs under control, left Scotland in order to go to London and thence to France, where he would soon be

King Edward I at the front of his men during the sacking of Berwick.

embroiled in a war with his overlord, Philip III.

Under the English yoke, the Scots, as devotees of the film *Braveheart* with Mel Gibson will understand, seethed with rancour. In 1297, William Wallace and Andrew Moray raised a revolt in Moray and the north of Scotland. They led an army south to Stirling Bridge, where Moray and Mel Gibson (sorry, William Wallace) smashed the English army and overran the south of Scotland.

Edward left France immediately, gathered an army and marched north to Scotland, where, assisted with a body of archers armed with the new weapon, the deadly longbow, smashed Wallace at Falkirk.

Almost ten years of invasion and civil war now engulfed Scotland, and not until 1305, at Perth, did Edward manage to establish a sort of peace with the Scots. In return for Edward holding the leading castles, the Scots were given a form of 'home rule'. In 1306 however, this happy state was shattered, as a result of the murder of John Comyn (relative of John Balliol) by Robert Bruce (grandson of the contender for the throne of Scotland) at Dumfries Cathedral. This murder, most likely long planned in advance, was the signal for a revolt against the authority of the ailing Edward.

The Bruce nearly miscalculated. Edward rose from his sickbed, marched north to Scotland, and watched while his armies shattered the supporters of the Bruce. Those who did not die in battle were hung at gallows erected in London and Berwick. One of the unlucky ones was the Earl of Atholl, a relative of Edward's as he was a Plantagenet born on the wrong side of the blanket, one of his ancestors being a bastard of King John. In commemoration of his –

The murder of John Comyn in Dumfries Cathedral in 1306.

admittedly diluted – Royal Blood, Atholl was hung from a gallows built forty feet high. The ailing Edward was said to have been greatly pleased to hear news of his demise.

The death of Edward on 7th July near Carlisle was a blessing for the Bruce, as the new king, Edward II, went on to earn a reputation as one of the most stupid kings in the history of England. He would spend the early part of his life in loading favours on his homosexual favourite, Piers Gaveston, and in quarrelling with his barons, who, it must be said, were a very undistinguished bunch.

This set of circumstances was favourable in the extreme to the Bruce, who proceeded to reconquer the whole of Scotland gradually. The catastrophic defeat, which he managed to inflict on Edward at Bannockburn in 1314, was really inevitable.

Despite this defeat, Edward, with obstinacy entirely typical of a Plantagenet in general, and of his father in particular, and with a lack of judgement which his father would never have shown, refused to make peace. To teach him the error of his ways, the Bruce began to launch a series of devastating raids into England led by his most deadly followers: his homicidal brother, Edward; his arrogant nephew, Thomas Randolph, the Earl of Moray, and the most able and effective of all, James Douglas 'the Black Douglas' of Border folklore.

From 1315-18, these three ravaged the lands of Yorkshire. Northallerton, Knaresborough, Boroughbridge and many other towns in the Vale of York were sacked. The conditions in some areas were almost as bad as in the years of the Norman yoke under William the Bastard. The northern lords repeatedly begged Edward to give them aid, but Edward refused to either make peace or recognise the Bruce as King of Scotland or to travel north and give his people succour. The nobles and commons of the north were left wondering what should happen in order for their king to come to their aid.

Then in 1318, the Bruce took Berwick.

Yorkshire's turn for action was about to arrive.

CHAPTER VII

Slain by the sword, slain by the waters: Battle of Myton 1319

There are many strange and tragic events in the military history of Yorkshire: the blood bath at Towton; the treachery at the battle of Wakefield; the apogee of the Kingdom of the Anglo-Saxons at Brunanburh. The most bizarre battle however, must be the strange incident that goes by the name of the Battle of Myton in 1319.

This came about as a result of the Bruce taking Berwick in 1318. There was nothing chivalrous about the affair, no nonsense about brave Knights racing into the breach, of arrows pouring in hails on the attackers and defenders; that typical mediaeval expedient, bribery and treachery took the city.

The taking of Berwick came as a shock to the English court. Not only did it mean that the last foothold of English rule in Scotland was now extinguished, but with this fortress in his hands, the Bruce was poised to launch more attacks on the northern shires of England. There was also the fact that Berwick was the first town that Edward's father, Edward I (Edward Longshanks) had taken in his invasion of Scotland in 1296. The thought of not being able to match up to his domineering father, must have caused even the feckless Edward some misgivings.

For once, Edward II was galvanised into action, and he managed to agree with his leading nobles and opponents to march north and retake the city. So it was, to the huge relief of the northern nobles and commons, that Edward together with his hated rival, his cousin and greatest landowner in the land, Thomas, the Earl of Lancaster, marched with the great men of his realm into the land of the Scots.

The campaign

The army, which advanced north in 1319, must have been a large one. Though not as large as the one at Bannockburn perhaps, it would have included men from the lands of the Earl of Lancaster, and most of the Royal estates. The English army reached the vicinity of the Scottish border, by the end of August 1319, since it is recorded

Siege of a town in the fourteenth century.

that the siege of Berwick lasted from the 8th to the 18th of September.

The siege of Berwick is recorded as one of the only two incidents in which the Bruce determined to make a stand against a fully mobilised English Army (Bannockburn being the other one).

The Bruce poured foodstuffs and men into the fortress, and placed several skilled engineers in the city. However, this was not the only arrow in his quiver. His main effort to relieve Berwick would be made not in Scotland, but in England. As soon as the Bruce heard that the English were approaching the frontier, he decided to launch the classic guerrilla tactic of raiding into the enemy's homeland and attacking his communications in order to turn the English army back.

Thus it was, that those heavenly twins Douglas and Moray, were sent on a raid into England to devastate the land and in general, create as much mayhem as possible. As early as the 5th September, the Scottish force rode past Carlisle down the Tyne valley, and proceeded to devastate the area round Tyneside, Durham and North Yorkshire.

According to at least two chronicles, the Brut and the Scalacronica, the Scottish intended to invade Yorkshire, capture Edward's queen, Isabella, and end the war at a stroke. As Queen Isabella was in residence in the city of York at that time, this idea has some credence, especially as the name of an English spy in the city, Edmund Darel, is mentioned. The story was that the spy intended to lead the Scottish to the city to capture the queen, but then confessed his story to the Archbishop of York, William Melton, and offered to lead the English to where the Scottish were.

The author must admit to finding this story a little confusing. How could a spy in York keep in touch with the Scots and tell them where the Queen was residing? How could he know where the Scottish would be at any given time, as the army which invaded the shire in 1319,

Twins Douglas and Moray returning from their raid over the border.

was a lightly-equipped mobile force, constantly on the move?

Be that as it may, the decision was taken to send the queen by boat by means of the Rivers Ouse and Trent to Nottingham. This was accomplished successfully. (This would be the second time Queen Isabella had had to flee before her husband's enemies. In 1312, her husband's infatuation with the Gascon Piers Gaveston, had caused a baronial revolt against the King. The King, in a decision which may have caused Isabella to have her husband murdered in 1327, abandoned Isabella to ride away with Gaveston. As the Queen was heavily pregnant

The wife of Edward II, Queen Isabella of France, had much to put with – not least being her husband's homosexual adventures.

Edward II.

The object of Edward II's true passion, Gascon pretty-boy, Piers Gaveston. Edward's court was not impressed by this relationship.

at the time, this act by her husband, must have caused her severe distress.)

The question now remained for the Archbishop, what could he do about the Scots?

Owing to the fact that the army now campaigning in Scotland would have taken away nearly all the men-at-arms in Yorkshire, and that on the 9th of September, Edward had ordered the militia of the shire to march to Berwick, the answer is, not very much. The prelate's predicament was compounded by the fact, that the Archbishop was then ordered by Edward to do something about the Scots then ravaging the county. Taking into account the fact that Edward, by ordering the militia out of the shire, had just denuded Yorkshire of troops, this decision, even by the rather low standards of Edward II, can only be described as somewhat wanting in logic.

What happened next would be the greatest tragi-comedy in the well-stocked larder of Yorkshire fiascos.

The Battle

The Archbishop, whom it appears possessed a great deal more bravery than brains (An English characteristic) was informed that the Scottish army was encamped 'secretly' at Myton-on-Swale about twelve miles north-west of York. How a large force encamped in the open can be defined as 'secretly' is beyond this author's comprehension.

On receiving this news, the worthy prelate, decided to march immediately to confront the Scots. The 'army' he led consisted of peasants, merchants, the Mayor of York, Sir Nicholas Fleming, the king's chancellor, John de Hothum, Bishop of Ely, the Abbots of Selby and Saint Mary, the Dean of York and the King's notary Andrew Tang. Just to ensure the sanctity of the army, and perhaps shout down curses on the godless Scottish, about 300 priests in full vestments also attended the march.

The army marched out of York, and travelled Northwest to Myton. Chroniclers give their strength at about 10,000. As at this time the whole of the population of York was about 9,000, this can be looked upon as the usual mediaeval inability to count large numbers. A figure of about 2,000 would seem to be reasonable.

It must have been about late afternoon, when this crowd (no other noun can be used here) approached the bridge at Myton-on-Swale, where the Scottish army lay 'secretly' encamped.

The chroniclers (including modern authors who should know better) have estimated the Scots at 15,000 men. As the whole of the Scottish army at Bannockburn was only 8,000, and since then a large number of Scots had

The Archbishop of York played a major role in the Battle of Myton.

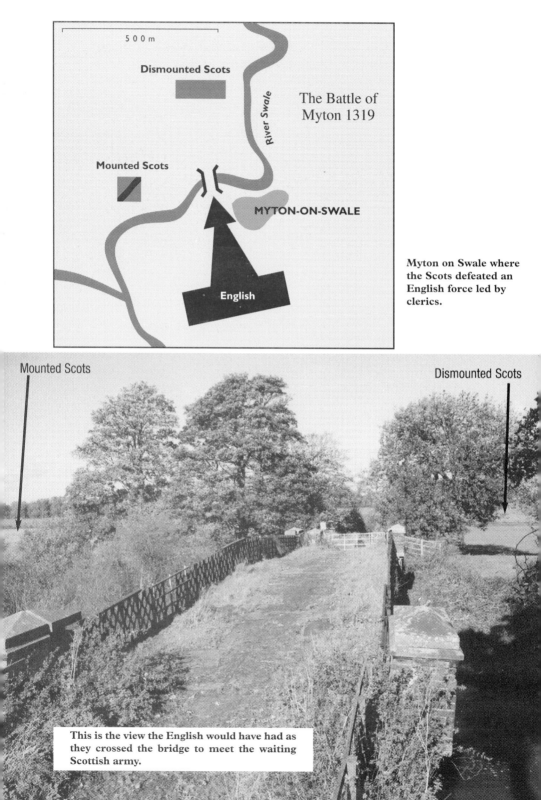

The Battle of Myton 1319

Myton on Swale where the Scots defeated an English force led by clerics.

This is the view the English would have had as they crossed the bridge to meet the waiting Scottish army.

The bridge that exists today was built on the site of the original crossing point of the Swale.

followed Edward Bruce to Ireland, once again we have a mediaeval computation error. Perhaps 1,500 men would be a more accurate estimation.

The sight of the Yorkshire crowd must have caused disbelief in the ranks of the Scottish force. An army used to continuous warfare, which had for at least the past ten years been used to a diet of uninterrupted success, led by two of the most lethal captains of the day, were facing a rabble of untrained husbandmen and merchants.

What happened next was nothing but inevitable.

According to the chronicler Nicholas Barbour, the Scottish force divided into two sections. One section dismounted and took position to the north of the Bridge. We are told they were in close order with shields linked and spears pointed towards the English. The other section was mounted, and, probably, took position to the west of the bridge.

The English crowd, who do not appear to have been aware of the basic concept of military operations, that of sending out mounted parties to scout out the opposition, was allowed to cross over the bridge unhindered.

The Scottish had fired three haystacks to the north of the bridge, with the result that, when they had crossed the crowd was engulfed in smoke. Coughing and choking, the English advanced to see the infantry of the northern wing of the Scots advancing upon them, shouting, according to the horrified chroniclers 'wild battle cries'. The English recoiled in terror from the advance, at which time the mounted wing of the Scots charged and crashed into the flank of the English. In an instant, the English crowd, was transformed into a terrified mob racing away from the Scots.

Unfortunately for them the mounted Scots had managed to cut off the retreat at the bridge, with the result that 'those who did not run, were killed by the sword, those who did, perished in the stream'. The Mayor of York was slain, as were at least 1,000 men, including almost 300 priests, which allowed the Scottish to give the whole incident the ghoulish, but not inaccurate name, of the 'Chapter of Myton'.

The Archbishop of York escaped owing it is said, to the swiftness of his horse, which also seems to show he did not reach the northern bank of the river. The man who bore his archbishop's cross, thinking common sense overcame sanctity, prudently dumped it, and ran for his life. A local peasant later discovered it, and, rather sacrilegiously, kept it. A most un-mediaeval prick of conscience however, later made him take it back to the unfortunate divine.

Epilogue

The action at Myton, is perhaps the greatest fiasco in military terms that the shire of Yorkshire has ever seen. It in no way hindered the Scottish in the plundering of the county, and, when the news eventually reached Berwick, the northern lords promptly broke off the siege and journeyed south to protect their lands. The only advantage, which accrued from this incident therefore, was entirely to the benefit of the Scots.

Thus we come to the end of this unfortunate chapter. (Do not think a pun intended, I entreat)

CHAPTER VIII

The Battle of Boroughbridge, 1322

The battle of Boroughbridge, had its genesis in the siege of Berwick in 1319. Upon hearing of the defeat of the Yorkshire 'army', and the ravaging of the shire, Thomas of Lancaster, proceeded to march to the south to protect his lands in Yorkshire and Lancashire. As he and his mesne made up at least one third of the Royal Army, Edward II had no choice but to break off the siege.

Edward was enraged over this incident, and the behaviour of Lancaster was criticised in more than one contemporary chronicle.

The fury and hatred which Edward bore to his cousin (there is really no other way now to describe their relationship), was if anything, increased over the next few months; Edward had always had a genius for offending his nobility. At his ascension, his raising of his homosexual favourite, the arrogant pretty boy, Piers Gaveston, to the Earldom of Cornwall and marriage into the Royal family, had enraged the nobility. The judicial murder of this strange creature, Piers Gaveston, and the presenting of his head to the Earl of Lancaster, was the start of the bitter feud between he and Edward.

Edward, not learning the lesson of Gaveston, almost immediately fell under the spell of the vain but able Baron Hugh Despenser. Edward proceeded to lavish gifts on this ruthless individual, who used his position to despoil any neighbour within reach of as much land as possible. The nobles of England, led inevitably by Lancaster, at a Parliament in 1321 insisted on the exile of Despenser, and a series of reforms to be enacted in the Royal household.

Faced with a near revolt, Edward, advised by the moderate Earl of Pembroke, and his wife, the French princess Isabelle, gave way on all matters. Despenser was exiled (an exile which he found rather exhilarating, as he spent some of his time in plundering shipping in the English Channel), and some reforms enacted. If this was not enough, Lancaster insisted, that as Steward of England – a position, incidentally, he did not hold – he had the right to appoint the king's advisers and to adjudicate on a number of incidents regarding the Royal household.

Edward was, understandably enraged over these demands, which could explain the strange incidents which now occurred.

In October 1321, Queen Isabelle decided to go on a pilgrimage to Canterbury Cathedral. She reached Leeds castle in Kent, a royal castle, held by the Steward of the Household, Bartholomew Badelsmere. The worthy Badelsmere was the equivalent of the mediaeval fence-sitter, as he had previously been sent on an embassy to the rebellious barons, and, to the fury of Edward, had become one of their number. This did not endear him to the Earl of Lancaster however, as Badelsmere held the stewardship of the household, the post Lancaster coveted. Lord Badelsmere was away at the time, and his wife, understandably in a panic as to what to do, knowing her husband was no longer one of the court party, panicked and shut the gates of the castle in the queen's face.

The queen, furious at this insult, promptly ordered her entourage, to attack the castle. This was done immediately, and seven of her followers were killed in the attempt. Anyone who has visited the castle and seen its natural strength will understand this.

The insult to the queen was one, which even Edward would not be able to stomach. In a suspiciously short period of time, a large army, including a contingent of Londoners and mercenaries, led by Edward, marched on the castle, which was taken quickly and it's garrison either hung or imprisoned.

Badelsmere had tried to raise support from the marcher lords of the Welsh march, who were the natural enemies of Edward, as Despenser had managed to seize a great deal of their lands. In company with Badelsmere, they marched to Kingston-upon-Thames, begging Lancaster for support. With the lack of perception which guided all his actions, Lancaster refused to come south, with the result that the Marcher lords, with Badelsmere in tow, fell back to the Welsh march.

Edward, intoxicated by his all too rare military success, proceeded to turn west and march to the Severn to punish the marcher lords for the treason. The lords of the march, realising that the wind had turned against them, once again begged

The siege of Carlise from the initial letter of the Charter of 1316, with (top left) the figure of Sir Andrew Harclay.

Lancaster for help. Lancaster once again did not come, passing the time by holding a series of northern parliaments which titillated his considerable self-esteem and by entering into treasonable correspondence with James Douglas, who described Lancaster in the letters they exchanged with the grotesquely inappropriate *nom de plume* 'King Arthur'.

The non-appearance of Lancaster was to the advantage of Edward, who throughout November and December, campaigned along the River Severn, taking the fortresses of his rebellious lords. Owing to the divisions in the enemy camp, Edward either imprisoned or drove away the most important marcher lords. By February, 1322, Edward held court in the town of Gloucester, having managed in a few short months completely to turn the tables on his enemies.

While in Gloucester, Edward was visited by the Warden of the West Scottish March, Sir Andrew Harclay. Harclay warned Edward that the Scottish, kept in check through a peace treaty signed several months previously and which lasted until 6th January, were once again on the rampage, and he begged Edward to come north with his army to oppose them.

Edward, probably thinking it was best to get rid of the wolf in his house than the ones in the fields, thanked Harclay, but insisted that he gather his men from the West March, and head south to entrap Lancaster.

Monument to the the 'Black' Douglas of border legend at Douglas, Scotland.

So it was, that early in the month of March, Edward advanced into Coventry to finish once and for all with his treacherous cousin, while Harclay advanced from the north to strike Lancaster in the rear.

Throughout the campaign of Edward on the Severn, Lancaster had done very little to improve his position, apart from holding a few northern parliaments, which achieved little and entering into treasonable correspondence with Robert the Bruce. These actions having achieved nothing at all, Lancaster, with marcher lord

Humphrey de Bohun, Earl of Hereford, a man known for more bravery than brains, together with the wretched Lord Badelsmere in tow, now decided to march south and confront the king with an army of mostly conscripted levies, who wanted nothing whatsoever to do with the action of their lord.

By early March, Edward faced Lancaster across the river Trent, whose swollen waters ensured that neither force could attack the other. Edward, showing a vigour in military affairs he had hidden, managed to cross the Trent further upstream, forcing Lancaster and an increasingly mutinous army to retreat to the north. Lancaster, it seems, put great faith in the abilities of his favourite knight, Sir Robert Holland, to recruit troops for him in his Earldom of Derby. Holland, seeing the way the wind was blowing, decided to act in a way any chivalrous knight and believer in loyalty would do in a situation like this: he deserted immediately to Edward.

The rebel army, now much reduced by desertions, retreated to Pontefract, the Earl's own castle. At a hurried council, some urged that they immediately retreat to the Earl's great castle at Dunstanburgh and beg the aid of the Scots. Lancaster refused to heed this prudent advice, idiotically claiming that if they marched to the castle, the king would think them traitors. It was not until Roger De Clifford actually threatened Lancaster with his sword, that Lancaster reluctantly gave the orders to march north.

The rebel army disconsolately retreated up the vale of York, over the bridge at Ferrybridge, toward Boroughbridge on the River Ure, a place which had already been sacked by the Scots in 1319.

Expecting to find some comfortable billets in the dwellings at Boroughbridge, the rebel army was appalled to find when they reached the area on 16th March that on the north bank of the river, was the army of Andrew Harclay.

Harclay had obeyed his king's orders with alacrity after his meeting with Edward in Gloucester. He had raised an army of knights and hobelars (mounted archers and light infantry) and had hurriedly marched southeast from Carlisle. The chroniclers state he had with him about 4,000 men, a number which is, by mediaeval standards, suspiciously low and which seems to give credence to its accuracy.

Harclay positioned his men with great care, which seems to show he had arrived earlier on the Ure. There were two places at which travellers could cross the Ure at this time: a narrow bridge which stands where the modern bridge is now located, and a ford a little to the east.

Harclay placed his footmen and knights at the northern end of the bridge and on the north side of the ford. He seems to have placed his archers on the flanks of the footmen. Harclay had, it seemed, adopted the tactics which would be used by the English armies in France in the 100 Years' War.

Lancaster must have been as shocked as Hardrada had been at Stamfordbridge. With the king marching on his rear, and with an army encamped to the north of the Ure, Lancaster's position can only be described as unenviable. As the river was now probably swollen with the waters of the winter thaw, any attack over the river would have been risky in the extreme. (Anyone who visits Boroughbridge, and seeing how steep the river banks are, can only concur with this)

Lancaster, whose army could not have been over 1,000 strong, and was probably a lot smaller, desperately tried to bribe and persuade Harclay to let him pass or join with him. With all the cards stacked in his favour, Harclay, not unnaturally refused.

With no other option open to him, Lancaster decided to attack.

It was agreed that the Earl of Hereford and Clifford, would lead their forces, on foot, on a direct attack on the Bridge, while Lancaster would lead some cavalry at the ford. (Or that swollen part of the river at which the ford was supposed to exist.)

Hereford and Clifford led their troops with a panache that was worthy of a better occasion. On approaching the bridge, they were

Boroughbridge. The place where Hereford and Clifford tried to cross the river. The mediaeval bridge would have been narrower and the river far deeper in March 1322.

Monument at Alborough,
which originally stood at
Boroughbridge, and is
believed to
commemorate the battle
which took place there in
1322.

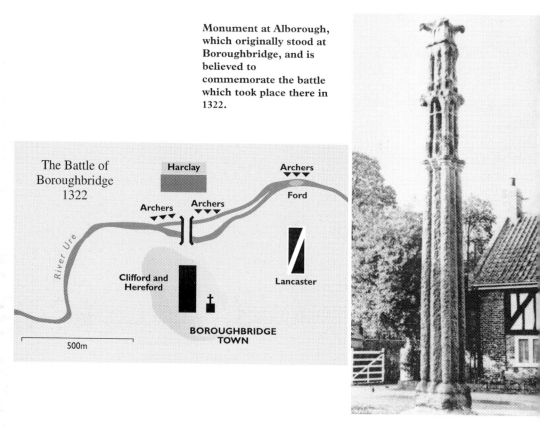

The Battle of
Boroughbridge
1322

Harclay

Archers

Ford

Archers   Archers

River Ure

Clifford and
Hereford

Lancaster

BOROUGHBRIDGE
TOWN

500m

hit by a fusillade of arrows which wounded Clifford and some other knights. Hereford bravely advanced through the arrow hail to the north of the bridge only to be promptly disembowelled by a Welsh spearman, who, in ignorance of the rules of chivalry, had lurked under the bridge and with incredible timing, had eviscerated the Earl with one thrust. Not unnaturally distressed by the injuries to their lords, the followers of Hereford and Clifford fell back.

At the ford, Lancaster had even less success; on nearing the spot, the archers of Harclay, opened such a shower of arrows, that he had to fall back. Lancaster could now think of nothing better to do than to arrange a temporary peace with Harclay. His troops, seeing the writing on the wall, began to desert.

Harclay, who was soon reinforced by the Sheriff of York, launched an attack the next day, and managed to seize Lancaster, Clifford and the wretched Badelsmere. What happened next must have been sweet

The Monument at Alborough, as it stands outside the Village Hall today, where its continued deterioration is evident when compared to the earlier picture opposite.

vengeance for Edward. Lancaster was led to his own castle of Pontefract, put on trial for high treason, refused permission to speak in his own defence, and, to the joy of the local populace, over whom Lancaster had been a viciously rapacious landlord found guilty and sentenced to be beheaded. To add insult to insult, Lancaster was paraded round the environs of Pontefract, where the delighted inhabitants pelted him with snowballs. He was taken to a small hillock, and, in direct imitation of the death of Gaveston, beheaded without a shred of legality, but much justice. To add injury to insult, more than one stroke was needed to separate his foolish head from his shoulders.

The executions did not stop there. The hapless Badelsmere, was taken to Canterbury, the original destination of Queen Isabelle, and there hanged. (Poetic justice?) Clifford was hung for treason at York. He would be the fourth member of his family in successive generations to die violently in the reign of Edward and his father.

The victory of Boroughbridge was due to many factors: the unnatural skill and energy Edward displayed in the campaign; Harclay's speed of movement, the natural strength of the Ure at that position and the numbers of the Royalist troops. Perhaps the most important reason would be the lethargy, indeed stupidity displayed by Lancaster, in delaying so long to do anything that smacked of common sense during the manoeuvres leading up to his defeat at Boroughbridge.

Edward was cock-a-hoop over his victory, which led him into a nearly fatal outburst of energy and confidence.

CHAPTER IX

Chicken hearted and luckless: Edward II and the Battle of Byland

Edward II, the son of the Hammer of the Scots, Edward I, has received a very bad press from historians. A homosexual who had a genius for quarrelling with many of his nobles; a man who was defeated in the most catastrophic defeat the English ever suffered before the fall of Singapore and after the battle of Hastings, (Bannockburn); a man who put all his trust in worthless favourites; a man who would be put to death in a brutal and appallingly sadistic manner at Berkeley Castle.

A fact which has gone unnoticed in all this however, is that the greatest military humiliation suffered by Edward, was not the battle of Bannockburn, but the incident generally unknown as the Battle of Byland.

Byland?

This infinitely obscure incident occurred in 1322, in an area northeast of Thirsk. The year in which this humiliating incident occurred did not begin too badly for Edward. In March of that year, owing to an upsurge of sympathy for him because of his wife, Isabelle of France (The French she-wolf) being publicly humiliated by a vassal of the Earl of Lancaster, Edward's cousin and main political foe, Edward had managed to gather an army to attack Lancaster and his ally, the earl of Hereford.

In an outburst of energy – unusual for him – Edward set off to meet his foes. Showing both caution and common sense (a near unique combination for any Plantagenet, something unheard of for Edward II) he managed to corner the two earls at Boroughbridge. Hereford was killed by being impaled by a spear, which a Welsh spearman, obviously not devotee of the proper arts of chivalry, thrust into a hole in the bridge Hereford was advancing over.

Lancaster, a man who was regarded as even more stupid, selfish and incompetent than Edward himself was taken alive, put on trial in his great hall of Pontefract, where, needless to say, his head soon parted company from his shoulders.

This defeat put Edward in a position of great power; not only had his two worst enemies in the kingdom been eradicated, but by confiscating a large part of their lands, he managed to make himself both temporarily solvent (a quite remarkable feat for the Plantagenets) but also gave him the strength to attack once again that bugbear of the first three Edwards, the Kingdom Of Scotland.

Since the great defeat at Bannockburn in 1314, Edward had not paid a lot of attention to northern affairs. The result of this, was that Robert the Bruce had been able to slowly tighten his grip on Scotland and to increase the amount of cash in the Scottish Exchequer by carrying out a series of ferocious raids into northern England,

Intoxicated by the victory of Boroughbridge, Edward, aided by the lands he had confiscated from the earldoms of Lancaster and Hereford, planned a campaign of omnipotence, and launched a huge army towards his northern neighbour in August 1322.

As was usual with Edward, luck did not attend his efforts. Due to a terrible outbreak of sheep and cattle murrain in northern England, together with a series of appalling harvests, the army had to march north on a shoestring logistics base. This was made worse when marching north of the Tees, the army (at least 20,000 strong by most estimates) entered a land that had been ravaged for years. The Bruce had given strict instructions that the land the English would march through be devastated.

The result was, when the English army arrived near Edinburgh in the middle of August, the land was reduced to a complete waste. The gods themselves were on the side of the Scots, for the fleet Edward had organised to supply the army with food, was scattered by a combination of bad weather and privateers. So appalling was the destruction, that all the English were able to capture, was one lame cow, bringing forth from the Earl of Warenne the comment, that 'yonder cow is the dearest piece of beef I have ever seen, as it has cost a thousand pound or more!'

The English army, in a quite severe state of privation, left the Kingdom of Scotland by the end of August, Edward himself going to Barnard Castle to lick his wounds. On the second of October, Edward headed south, which was almost the same time as the Bruce struck. On the 30th September, the Bruce invaded England through the West March at Carlisle.

Why did he attack on the west of the Pennines, and why did he not attack the English army as it reeled back through the Lothian and the East March?

An entry in the Lanercost Chronicle explains this. It states that the

Robert the Bruce memorial on the Bore Stone, Bannockburn.

Bruce had been kept informed by spies of the state of the English army, and that the army had been grossly reduced in size and Edward's personal entourage was very small. The Bruce probably waited till the English army had all but dissolved and decided to strike at the time when Edward was weakest.

As to why he invaded the western march rather than the eastern: perhaps he realised that the devastated nature of the eastern invasion route made it difficult to launch a raid the like of which he intended; perhaps he knew that if he invaded in the east, the English garrisons to be found on the frontier would give Edward news of his approach; perhaps he wanted to devastate the land of Carlisle, whose lord, Andrew Harclay had rebuffed him at the siege of Carlisle in 1315. What is known is that the Bruce spent about five days in ravaging the area around the city, leaving the vicinity on the 5th October.

The Lanercost Chronicle states that the Bruce intended to capture

Edward while he was still in the North. The fact the Bruce stayed in the Carlisle area for such a long time, was perhaps either to lull Edward into a false sense of security, or to provision his army for the stroke he was now to pull.

On 5th October, the Bruce led the Scots from Carlisle and swept southeast up the Eden valley. By the 13th October, they were at Northallerton. In eight days, the Scottish army had travelled about 100 miles, over the Pennine Hills and placed themselves in the heartland of north Yorkshire. This is a march that shows the ability of the Bruce to move quickly when he so desired, and seems to show the skill of the spies (in reality mounted mosstroopers) who kept him informed of the movements of Edward..

Since 2nd October, Edward had journeyed south to the abbey at Rievaulx, a few miles to the east of Thirsk. He was at the abbey when he was told that the Scottish were at Northallerton, less than twenty miles away.

At this stage it is important to understand the size and composition of the two armies, as if we do not, we will not be able to make sense of what happened next. The army of the Scots that fought at Bannockburn 1314 was around 14,000 strong. This was an army that the Bruce had been able to take considerable time over gathering, and we can assume it was the optimum total of the troops available to the Scottish at that time.

Though the Kingdom of Scotland had enjoyed some peace from this time onwards, taking into account the fact that the Kingdom as a whole was devastated, and that in 1315, Edward Bruce had led a large army into Ireland, the army Robert Bruce led into England in 1322 could not have exceeded 8,000 men, and was most likely a good deal smaller. Taking into account the fact that the march into Yorkshire over the Pennines must have been a severe one, this author thinks that the total number of Scots in the Northallerton vicinity, could not have been over 6,000.

It should be pointed out that the Lanercost Chronicler specifically mentions the Bruce brought with him men from the Western Isles and the Highlands on this raid. Taking into account this piece of information and the fact that the speed of the march from Carlisle was very impressive, we are left with the impression the Scottish army was a lightly armed and highly mobile army made up mostly of mounted troops. These men can be described as being hobelars – lightly armed horsemen, whose name is taken from the word 'hobin' meaning a light horse. Apart from the leading nobles, the Scottish army would be either totally unarmoured, or   wore protection leather, not the more substantial metal armour.

We can furthermore conclude that the army was in both a mood for revenge, and possessed of a high morale. The numerous campaigns it had endured over the previous few years, together with a run of almost unbroken success, would have meant that the army would have 'gelled' together. This is an important fact to consider when studying the battle that was about to be fought.

Of the English army, we can only say it must have been substantially smaller than the Scottish. It seems that Edward had only three earls with him at the time: the Earls of Richmond, Louth and Pembroke. The Earl of Louth, John of Bermingham, had been in command of the army which had defeated the army of Edward Bruce, Robert Bruce's headstrong younger brother at Fochart in 1318. Edward Bruce would be the fourth of the brothers of the Bruce to die violently at the hands of the English. It is also to be noted that a large deputation of foreign knights was with Edward on a diplomatic mission. This seems to show that the appearance of the Scottish army had come as a complete shock to Edward and his advisers.

The 14th October saw the Scots advancing east from Northallerton to attack Edward. This decision to attack once the location of the English army was noted substantiates the belief that the Scottish were trying to capture Edward himself, and must show the Bruce in a bold light as a commander to advance ten miles to the east and attack his enemy immediately.

This is the view the Scots would have had as they approached the English army lined up along the top of Hambleton Hills. Even at this distance the hills look to be a formidable obstacle.

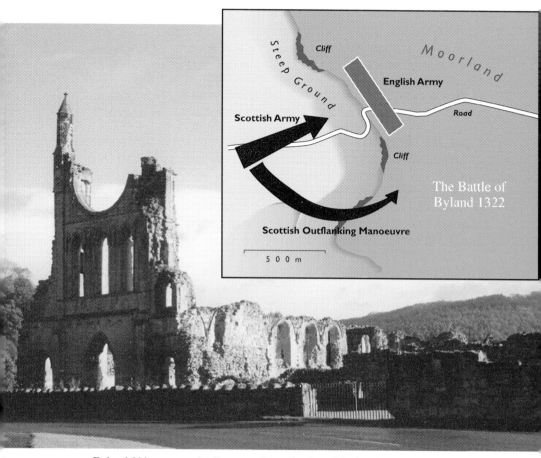

Byland Abbey, several miles away from the site of the battle, but one of the few remaining bits of evidence indicated on a present-day map to identify the location of Byland.

Given these facts, the tactical dispositions the English adopted can be described as being only too necessary.

According to the historian G. Barrow, the English army took position on the Western edge of Scawton Moor. As can be seen by any ordnance survey map, they occupied a steep and strong position, which given a resolute and large army, would have proven to be near impregnable.

The chronicler John Barbour, however, states that the English held the position, to give Edward time to escape. This statement seems to show that the army of the English, or at the very least its leaders, had no faith in the outcome, and must confirm this author's belief in that the English army was grossly outnumbered.

The Bruce ordered the Earls of Douglas and Moray to attack straight up the heights of Scawton Moor, and sent his highlanders to the flanks of his army, ordering them to scale the crags adjoining the English positions.

The result was inevitable. Pressed on the front by the Scottish, and assailed on the flanks by the highlanders, the English army collapsed, in ruin. The Earl of Richmond and some of the French knights were captured, together with the Knights Thomas Uhtred and Ralph Cobham, the latter of which must have been a doughty fighter, as he was regarded as the best knight in England For a second time Edward II lost all his baggage and equipage. (He lost his personal shield, which the Bruce was polite enough to return to him.) Some reports state that the Scots pursued Edward to the very gates of York itself, after a long and circular tour to escape his pursuers.

The defeat at Byland, was in most contemporaries' eyes, a worse humiliation than Bannockburn. The author of the Vita Edward Secundii, bitterly berated the monarch for undertaking a campaign that led to such terrible results. The Bridlington Chronicler, with brutal frankness, accused Edward of being 'chicken hearted and luckless in war'. The collapse in faith regarding the king would be a major factor in the success of the invasion by his wife, Isabelle a few

The English army had positioned itself along the escarpment at Byland, which is today known as Sutton Bank. The A170 climbs up the hill to the English position.

English

years later, and for his appalling death in Berkeley castle.

Though Edward may be berated for his defeat, the main reasons for the English defeat at Byland, are surely the skills displayed by the Bruce. By waiting at Carlisle to ensure the English army had practically disintegrated before he advanced together with the bold and speedy march through the Pennines, shows the Bruce to have been a strategist both bold and cautious.

The decision to attack Edward as soon as he heard of his whereabouts, together with the tactical plan he devised as soon as he saw the (admittedly, grossly outnumbered English army) on the heights above him, proves the Bruce to have been able to make a snap judgement based on the facts at hand, while his plan of attack, a frontal charge aided by a flanking movement, show him to be one of the great captains of the time, and certainly, the greatest warrior the Scots have ever produced.

Looking from the English position across the Vale of York. The road follows the main route taken by Robert the Bruce in his assault on the English. Sutton Bank is steep enough to warrant the banning of caravans on this section of the road.

CHAPTER X

𝔓eaceful period – well, almost

Apart from a campaign in 1327, famous mostly for the fact that a group of English archers and Hainault mercenaries came to blows over a game of dice in York, the county of Yorkshire did not see any large-scale fighting with the Scots over the next few years. The deposition of Edward II formulated by his wife, Isabelle, and her paramour, Roger Mortimer, in 1327, together with Edward's brutal and degrading death in Berkeley castle, allowed more rational minds to conduct England's affairs. In 1328, the treaty of Edinburgh, ratified at Northampton, gave the Scots their right to be acknowledged as a totally independent entity, and recognised the Bruce as the rightful king of Scotland.

This state of affairs was not long to last, as the new king, Edward III, proved to be just as intransigent, and far more able than his father. Throughout his life, Edward would be campaigning against the Scots and the French, in a quest for what would turn out to be cloud-cuckoo ambitions for thrones in Scotland and France.

Edward II in a state of collapse upon his threatened removal as king. His abdication was called for by the nobles, in favour of his son, following his years of mismangement of affairs of state. He was brutally murdered at Berkley Castle (left) after his son Edward III took the throne.

Though the years of Edward III's reign would see campaign after campaign being organised, Yorkshire saw no fighting over its own land. The coming of the Black Death in 1349 certainly brought death, but little destruction to the shire. Edward III, the victor of Crécy and Halidon Hill, died a bitter and broken senile, old man in 1377, the slave of his mistress, Alice Perrers, and bereft of his eldest son, Edward the Black prince, who had died before him. Edward's grandson, Richard of Bordeaux, succeeded to the throne as a minor in 1377. It would be thanks to this character, that Yorkshire would once again become a hotbed of strife.

Richard was in many respects a typical and atypical Plantagenet. He was arrogant and self-centered (nothing strange about that) rude to his servants (not really strange) loved fine and extravagant clothes (the Plantagenets were not really fashion models in

Edward III.

this respect) and a pronounced lover of literature (now that was strange). He was also untrusting and untrustworthy, autocratic, and for years was in thrall to his favourite, the worthless Earl of Oxford.

At first dominated by his uncles, as he grew older, Richard threw off their hold over him, and had both the Earl of Gloucester, and the Earl of Arundel murdered, then he banished the Duke of Norfolk and the Duke of Lancaster.

Richard's increasingly autocratic and unstable manner soon made him a figure of fear and hatred among most classes of the English. His cousin, the Duke of Lancaster, Henry of Bolingbroke, returned from his exile and invaded England, landing at Ravenspur in 1399. So hated was Richard, that Bolingbroke was able to march almost

Richard II

unopposed to London. Richard at this time, was trying to quell a revolt in Ireland, and had left England in the hands of his Uncle, Edmund Duke of York. Edmund, as any loyal follower of a king, was more concerned with keeping his head on his shoulders than dying for Richard, and showed himself to be a political weathercock, allowing Bolingbroke to enter London and proclaim himself King.

Richard, on returning to England, saw his support vanish almost overnight, was captured, and put in confinement in Pontefract. Like his distant uncle, Thomas of Lancaster, Richard soon found out that Pontefract was an unlucky place for a loser, and was probably murdered there soon after.

Bolingbroke was able and energetic, and needed to be, as he was soon involved in a brutal war against the ever-rebellious Welsh. To make things worse, Bolingbroke had stumbled onto a problem which would prove to be both intractable and unlovable. Bolingbroke was the son of John of Gaunt, the third son of Edward III. The second son of Edward however, Lionel of Antwerp, had left as his heir, a daughter, Phillippa, who had married Edmund Mortimer, Earl of

Pontefract Castle, a lethel prison for losers of mediaeval times.

March. Their son, Roger, had probably been recognised as heir presumptive by Richard.

The fact that he would have lost his head if he had tried to claim the throne from Bolingbroke, persuaded Mortimer to keep quiet. This would prove to be a wise precaution, as Bolingbroke showed himself, like any mediaeval king, to be very sensitive to charges that he had usurped the throne.

The noble and rather foolish house of Percy, who had helped Henry IV (as we should now call him) gain the throne, soon turned against him. At the battle of Shrewsbury in 1403, the Percys under the leadership of Hotspur Percy, lost not only the battle, but Hotspur and his uncle, the Earl of Worcester, were killed in the action.

The head of the Percy clan, Henry Percy, Earl of Northumberland, had fallen ill during the campaign, and managed to keep his body in one piece. When questioned by Henry as to his knowledge of his son's treason, Percy senior replied that he had known nothing about it. Even by the standards of the time, this was a disingenuous answer, but Henry IV, being a realist, accepted it. Though Percy was imprisoned for a while, he was restored to his estates, and, not learning the lesson, immediately began plotting again. In 1405, together with Thomas Mowbray and Archbishop Scrope of York, Northumberland raised an army and Henry IV was once again faced with the prospect of fighting a battle as bloody as Shrewsbury.

What happened next is an episode in Yorkshire history, which has more in common with *The Prince* by Machiavelli, than fights between honest and noble Englishmen.

Though the Percys were very powerful in the north, and had been hereditary Wardens of the East March of England, they had lately acquired rivals in the area, in the family of the Nevilles, whose current head, Ralph, the Earl of Westmoreland, would prove to possess a cunning and a lack of scruple, together with a pretty shrewd idea as to where the power of the land lay, attributes which would be lacking to a disastrous degree in his descendants.

Henry IV

Lord Neville approached the army of the rebels at Shipton Moor, with a much smaller force. By sheer cunning, he persuaded the somewhat unworldly Scrope to disband his forces and promised to redress the rebels' grievances. Scrope, to the horror of his more realistic supporters, did so, and a little later, was arrested with them, by Westmoreland, who had merely used this despicable but highly effective way to get the rebel leaders in his power.

When Henry got his hands on these deluded creatures, there was no option open to him but to execute them. Mowbray and the laymen were executed as traitors. Scrope, though a cleric, was also executed. His blood was technically inviolable being an Archbishop, five strokes of the executioner's axe proved otherwise however. (Henry, to the delight of the Clerical chroniclers, who so repeatedly misinform the general leader, later contracted a disease, which has been variously described as leprosy or syphilis, for ordering this only too-necessary act) Scrope's tomb – inevitably – soon became a place of pilgrimage, and the usual mendacious miracles were noted there.

There would be only one more military incident in the reign of

Archbishop Scrope being prepared for execution for treason against his lord and King, Henry IV, at York, 1405.

Henry IV: the final fling of the unlucky Earl of Northumberland. Having gone into exile in Flanders following the foolish affair at Shipton Moor, Northumberland travelled to Scotland to raise an army of Scottish and Percy retainers, to overthrow the rather unstable throne of Henry IV. In their march down into Yorkshire, this somewhat strange army, gathered into its ranks more clerics than soldiers. At Bramham Moor, on February 19th, the rebels met the Yorkshire levies under Thomas Rokeby, the Sheriff of Yorkshire. Northumberland was killed in the battle, and some of the foolish clerics hung.

Yorkshire for the rest of the reign would be at peace.

The Earl of Westmoreland, Ralph Neville, the conqueror of John Scrope the Archbishop of York.

CHAPTER XI

The Wars of the Roses: violence, treachery and slaughter

Though the Wars of the Roses initially broke out in 1453, their genesis begins in the reign of Henry IV, when the Percys were beaten and their estates confiscated. The main beneficiaries of this change in circumstances would be the Neville Earls of Westmoreland. Ralph of Westmoreland, by his marriage to Henry IV's sister, and the acquiring of Percy estates, managed to begin a feud which would have catastrophic consequences for both houses later on. Neville's begetting of a huge family would lead to some rather strained family relationships.

Under the reign of Henry V, who with William the Conqueror and Richard the Lionheart is one of the three truly savage and sadistic kings in English history, Yorkshire was at peace, Henry discovering it was more profitable to murder innocent French peasants in Normandy, then kill his own people in England.

Henry V's death in France, in 1422, came as a huge relief to the French, and to the distress of the English, who had now the infant Henry VI as king, and a pack of rather unruly and foolish nobles, particularly Henry Duke of Gloucester, and Cardinal Beaufort as regents.

Henry V, the bellicose ruler of England 1413 to 1422. His tendency to make war against the French meant a period of calm on the Home Front.

To the surprise of many observers, the first few years of the Regency of Henry VI, was remarkably quiet. The nobles and clergy (read Gloucester and Beaufort) ruled efficiently and well, and it would not be till the 1440s, that affairs began to take a turn for the worse. The reason for this can be laid at two doors: the war in France and the character of young Henry VI. His father, the murderous Henry V had given the hundred years' war a new, and a much more savage direction. By invading and plundering France, Henry had managed to unite his subjects behind

Joan of Arc, on top of the scalling ladder, claimed to hear voices directing her to take up arms against the invaders. Her endeavours in rallying the French succeeded in making the presence of the English in that country extremely costly. From the point of view of the English the sooner she could be caught and burnt the better.

him, and take into the continent all the more disgruntled and violent sectors of the populace. These feats managed to make the kingdom of England a haven of peace and prosperity for the time being.

However, with the coming of Joan of Arc together with the powerful duke of Burgundy casting in his lot with the new French king, Charles VIII, France turned from a place to be milked to a country into which resources had to be poured for no effective return. France became a serious drain for 15th Century England. The demands for more and more money to prosecute the war would soon inspire a great deal of anger amongst the English.

Henry VI must take the blame for the unfortunate slide into civil war that got under way as he left his teens behind. He appears to have been a man, who, though not mentally subnormal, was at least a rather dim and foolish individual. Throughout his life he appeared to take very little interest in affairs of state, his advances into the political arena, being confined to occasionally sitting in judgement in the law courts and giving mercy to the most hardened and desperate criminals, his idea being that a king should be merciful at all times.

This most un-Plantagenet characteristic did not sit well with either the nobles or the commons, who began to look upon him as a fool.

It is to be noticed that the breakdown in law and order which seemed to take place in the years before the wars of the Roses seemed to start in the 1440s, when Henry, now in his early twenties, should have been taking over the administration of the realm. Unfortunately,

Henry did nothing of the sort, and proceeded to spend most of his time in praying and doing everything his priests told him to do.

In 15th Century Christendom, a kingdom who had a king who refused to rule was like a ship with no rudder. The governance of the realm soon came into the hands of royal favourites, such as the Dukes of Suffolk and Somerset, whose ideas seemed to be limited to lining their own pockets as fast as they could, in a manner which seemed rapacious even by the standards of the English.

This situation was not improved by the marriage of Henry, to the French princess, Margaret of Anjou, in 1445. This wedding had been arranged in order to confirm a peace which had been hammered out by Suffolk and Somerset, who realised that the English presence in France was not a viable option.

Unfortunately, Suffolk, the guiding force behind the treaty, was forced to offer such huge concessions that even his own party was appalled at them. To make matters worse, the marriage to Margaret was discovered to be rather one-sided; so poor was her father, the dreamy Rene of Provence, that no dowry accompanied Margaret, and, indeed, Suffolk even had to pay the costs of the wedding.

The marriage was a mixture of fire and water; Henry, overwhelmed by his wife's beauty and intelligence, soon became her complete disciple. Margaret was a very able, tempestuous and rather narrow-minded woman, who saw in her role

Henry VI married Margaret of Anjou – a weak monarch and a beautiful, strong-minded woman. The stage was set for warring and feuding that would later be called Wars of the Roses.

as queen that of a partner and assistant which was wholly foreign to the xenophobic English.

The marriage of Margaret and Henry seemed to be the signal for a riot of anarchy to sweep England. In the north, the Percy family, still seething over the confiscation of some of their estates by the Nevilles in the Percy revolts, could only look on in anger as the huge brood of Ralph of Westmoreland (he, or rather his two wives had twenty- three Children), proceeded to claw their way further up the ladder of success, by marrying nearly every eligible heiress and heir in sight. In the south, in a wave of popular revolt not seen even in the peasants' rebellion, a revolt, led by a certain Jack Cade, whose rise seemed to be solely due to the fact that everyone was sick and tired of the anarchy which now reigned over parts of England, marched on London.

Though this revolt was eventually put down, victims galore would die as result of it. The Duke of Suffolk was taken at sea where he was trying to flee to Flanders, by a ship whose crew greeted him with the jovial cry of 'Welcome traitor'. Charged with treason and bad governance of the realm, he was immediately beheaded. One Suffolk's main advisers, Adam Moleyns, Bishop of Chichester, was murdered by a disgruntled mob of seamen and soldiers, who killed him for a rather more prosaic reason: they thought that he had embezzled their wages.

Though Cade's revolt was put down, the whole country seemed to be ill at ease and waiting for a man to follow. This man, one of the most unlucky in English history, would be Richard the Duke of York.

As a man who was descended from both the second and fourth of the sons of Edward III, York could be claimed to have an even better right to the throne than Henry himself. He was regarded, it seems, as heir presumptive to the English throne until Margaret in 1453, produced a son, Edward. Given the fact that Henry VI had a morbid dislike of both sex and nudity, it is not surprising that from the very beginning doubts were raised as to the child's paternity. The Duke of Somerset is the one usually suggested as being the father.

For the first years of his life, York, whom as a child the Nevilles had brought up owing to the fact his father, Richard of Cambridge had been executed for treason, had served Henry quite well; he had been the King's lieutenant in France on two occasions, served as governor of Ireland and fulfilled these duties with energy and honesty if with not much glory.

Unfortunately, as a great nobleman, York had to pay the wages of a large part of the men under his command. As the Royal Government, now dominated by the Duke of Somerset, refused to pay him, York, to his fury, was saddled with series of debts he could not pay. His fury increased in 1447, when he was appointed governor of Ireland. To his disgust he had to turn the French lands over to the new governor, none other than the Duke of Somerset. Insult to injury was added when he learned that the Duke of Somerset took up his new post with £25,000 to pay the wages of the troops. This while he, York, was sent to the backwater of Ireland with two years' pay owing.

The rule of York in Ireland was so wise, that for years, the Irish regarded the York dynasty as 'their' ruling family. Despite the loyalty of the Irish, York's stay in Ireland was a frustrating one, as his rival, the Duke of Somerset, was literally blasted out of France by the French army, equipped with the new cannons which would soon dominate warfare.

In 1452, so angered was York at his treatment, that, gathering a small force, he marched to London to demand the dismissal of the Duke Of Somerset from the King's council. Meeting the king at Blackheath, he was invited to the king's presence to discuss the matter. He accepted the offer, dispersed his army – to find Somerset at Henry's side. York was forced to make a grovelling apology, and ride like a criminal before Henry on the way to London.

York retired to his estates following this fiasco, to ponder on what to do next. He did not have long to wait, as in 1453, Henry VI had a complete mental breakdown, which wrecked whatever consensus there was at the Royal Council. To make things worse, the ever-smouldering Neville-Percy feud broke out again. At Heworth Moor, the two families nearly fought a battle when a party of the Percy faction ambushed a bridal party of the Neville faction. Though the ambush was beaten off, the fact that such an incident could occur miles away from the march where both families were supposed to be fighting the Scots is indicative of the state of affairs that then existed.

The York-Somerset feud, and the clash between the Nevilles' and the Percies, became even more complicated a little later. The Duke of York was married to Cecily Neville, the youngest of the Northumberland brood; also, the Duke of Somerset was granted some lands in south Wales, which the council did not appear to have observed was already in the hand of Richard Neville, Earl of Warwick and the Brother-in law of York.

Warwick, the famous 'Kingmaker' of Shakespeare, was the last person to actually allow the hated Somerset take over lands he regarded as his. A deal was struck between York on the one hand, and Warwick and his father, the Earl of Salisbury

The heraldic representation of Richard Neville, Earl of Warwick. He was arguably the most powerful man in the kingdom as Henry VI took the throne.

on the other. It was simplicity itself. In return for their help against Somerset, York would help them against the Percys.

Over the next few months, tension rose visibly in the kingdom, an atmosphere that was in no way assuaged by the return to sanity of Henry VI. He promptly released Somerset from the Tower, where York and Co. had placed him during his 'illness'. York and the Neville faction promptly raised their affinities, marched on London, to confront Somerset. They were careful to make it clear that they were not raising arms against the king.

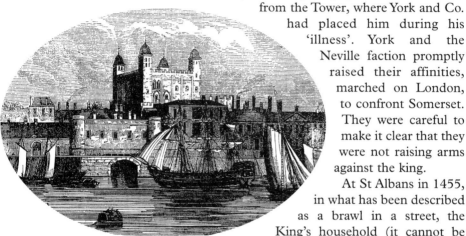

The Tower of London

At St Albans in 1455, in what has been described as a brawl in a street, the King's household (it cannot be described as an army) was routed. Among the dead were the Duke of Somerset (enemy of York and Warwick) Percy, Earl of Northumberland (enemy in general of the Nevilles) and Lord Clifford (direct descendant of that unlucky family at Boroughbridge, cousin and friend of the Percys, and therefore, enemy of the Nevilles). The fact that after these three were killed, the battle ended, shows not only how vicious the feuds of the time had now become, but how little the wars of the Roses had to do with national politics and how much more with Mafia-like family quarrels.

York and his faction ruled uneasily for several months, when the King resumed control of affairs, and the tensions, which had fallen slightly after Saint Albans, rose again. In 1459, the king, at the behest of the irrepressible Margaret decided to hold a Parliament, from which York and the Nevilles were conspicuously omitted.

Thinking the worst, York and Salisbury decided to march to Ludlow on the Welsh march, and concentrate their forces there.

Margaret and the followings of the Percys and Somerset (the son of the man killed at St Albans) pursued them there, and, aided by the fact that the garrison of Calais, brought over to England by the new Captain of Calais, Warwick, deserted to them, had the satisfaction of seeing the 'Yorkists' (to use a popular but very incorrect description) flee, Warwick and Edward of March, York's eldest son, and the Earl of Salisbury, to Calais, York and his younger son, the Earl of Rutland, to Ireland.

The next few months would see some kaleidoscopic changes in England: at a Parliament held in Coventry, York and the Neville faction were, not surprisingly, attained (that is, declared outlaws and their property confiscated); York made himself into the Governor of Ireland with ease, and ruled even better; Warwick took command of Calais, where he paid off the arrears of the garrison still ensconced there with a little piracy.

In 1460, Warwick, with surprising ease, which seemed to show just how unpopular the government of the Somerset's had been, invaded England, marched on to London, meeting no opposition worth the name, and seized the city with little effort. On 10th July, at the battle of Northampton, owing to the fact that one third of the King's army deserted him, Warwick overthrew the group of lords which can be called 'Lancastrian', who surrounded Henry VI. By the standards which followed, the fact that only four peers were killed or executed, shows just how much hesitation there was at this time to shed blood.

The 'Yorkists', who had captured Henry for a second time, promptly departed to London to await the arrival of the Duke of York. Though the battle of Northampton had been fought in July, York, for some reason, only landed in England at Chester in September.

York must have been a very frustrated man by now; he had repeatedly tried to show his loyalty to Henry, only to be rebuffed by the Somerset/Percy clique. The battle of St Albans had got him nowhere, and the flight from Ludford Bridge, must have shattered whatever confidence he had in the king. The fact that his nephew and son had taken Henry, and were ruling England, must have jarred on his nerves. The steps he now took, show either a man who had lost touch with reality, or one who had been misled by his own side as well.

After landing at Chester, where his wife, the indomitable Cecily, Neville joined him, York made a leisurely journey through England. He ordered the Royal Arms of England to be borne in front of him, and that a naked sword be held, upright, before him (for the uninitiated, these were the sole prerogatives of a king). Entering London 10th October, he marched into the great hall at Westminster, to the chamber where the king was accustomed to meet parliament. He put his hand on the cushion on the throne, and turned to look at the peers, nobles and commons looking at him.

To be greeted with a shocked silence.

York, by his behaviour, had made a formal claim for the throne. Given the fact that he and Warwick must have been in communication for weeks beforehand, either York did not inform the members of his own party that he intended to claim the kingship, or Warwick at the last minute could not bring himself to overthrow Henry. Led by the Archbishop of Canterbury, York was ushered away to 'discuss' the matter. York claimed the throne by reason of his superior descent from Edward III; as none of the nobles present, had any desire to overthrow Henry, this claim was embarrassing to say the least.

It was not until 24th October that a compromise was reached, which was obviously painful on all sides: Henry would be king for his lifetime, York would succeed to the throne on his death, while his family was considered to be the heirs of the kingdom.

Given the fact that Henry was twelve years younger than York, and that he was in good health, York appears to have bid an unhappy farewell to the crown. From this date, York now appears to have been outshone in the council by his son, Edward, the Earl of March, and his nephew, Warwick.

Though Henry – as usual – meekly accepted these conditions, they were ignored by his fiery queen, Margaret, who, since Northampton, had been in conclave with the northern lords, Northumberland and Clifford (both of whose fathers had been killed at St Albans), and was busily raising an army from the wild northlands, and ravaging the estates of both the Earl of Salisbury and the Duke of York.

The news of this gathering of enemies, could not have been of good cheer to the York faction; the news that the Duke of Somerset, now returned from France, and the Earl of Devon were marching to Yorkshire to aid Northumberland, would have made worse a very grave situation.

The scene was set for a bloodbath in Yorkshire, which has no parallel in English history.

CHAPTER XII

Battle of Wakefield 1460: the revenge of young men

The news of the gathering of enemies in Yorkshire must have caused the Yorkist affinity to realise that if their family were to get the throne, and the Nevilles to dominate the north, the 'Lancastrians' would have to be crushed once and for all. It was decided that the Earl of March, Edward, York's eldest son, would be sent to the Welsh march in order to raise troops. Warwick would remain behind in order to rule London, while York and Salisbury would march north to crush the Lancastrian forces.

On 9th December 1460, York and Salisbury marched north to Yorkshire. Their army has been estimated to have been about 5,000 strong, but for reasons, which will be explained later, was probably a lot smaller. As York and Salisbury must have realised they would be dealing with the Percy and Clifford affinities, together with the men of Somerset and Devon, it seems very strange indeed that they did not wait to recruit more men.

As their army marched in the middle of winter, the gathering of supplies, always the weak point of a mediaeval army, became very difficult. The train of artillery with the army had to be abandoned owing to the difficulty of its transport. At Worksop, the scouts of the Yorkist army appeared to have fought a skirmish with their Lancastrian counterparts, and when they marched into the castle of Sandal, a little south of Wakefield, the army must have been both tired and dispirited.

The situation facing York and Salisbury, as anyone who has visited the small castle of Sandal will appreciate, was now a very unpleasant one. Owing to the season of the year, and the fact that the estates of York and Salisbury in the vicinity had been either ravaged or overrun by the army of Northumberland and Clifford, their army was faced with a distinctly unpleasant supply crisis. Furthermore, by just looking from the battlements of Sandal castle, at the panoramic view to the north, it would have been obvious to all of the numbers of Lancastrian forces now in the area. Anyone who visits the castle now can appreciate the sight the Yorkists would have had from the walls.

Model of Sandal Castle as the stronghold would have appeared in the 15th Century.

The area to the north is level and mostly unwooded. York and Salisbury must have been told by their local tenants of the size of the armies against them. They included the affinities of Northumberland and the Percy faction, the Clifford affinity, and those of Somerset and Devon, together with a number of other northern families. The army of the Lancastrians, must have been at least 12,000 strong.

It should also be stressed, that the leaders of the army of Queen Margaret (we cannot call it the army of Henry VI) were for the most part, the sons of those men killed at St Albans. The combat, which would follow, would be famous for the Mafia-like vendettas, which had now been allowed to come to the boil by men thirsting for revenge.

With their forces outnumbered and hungry, with most of their men sleeping rough outside the castle. So small is Sandal, that 200 men would have caused overcrowding. The situation of York and Salisbury was bleak. If they stayed where they were, they would soon be forced to move to gather supplies to prevent starvation. This would mean that they would be advancing to meet a far superior army. They could retreat, and allow the Lancastrians to overrun the rest of the York estates, thus seriously reducing the men that Richard Duke of York could raise in future. Moreover, they would then be forced to retreat south over a route already eaten bare.

It was at this point that York seemed to get a break; it appears that a Christmas truce was arranged between the two forces which was to last till epiphany (6th January). A member of the numerous Neville clan, John Neville, got news to Richard that he was approaching with his affinity to help him. Phil Haigh, the acknowledged expert on the wars of the Roses, who very kindly took this author on a visit round the battlefield to describe what could have happened, states, and this author agrees with him, that this news was the direct cause of the Battle of Wakefield.

The news that Neville was marching to Sandal to help Richard would have brought the beleaguered Duke great peace of mind, since by the end of December, his supply situation must have been acute. Here we can see the mind of schemer Andrew Trollop, the Calais captain, who had joined the Lancastrians after Ludford Bridge.

The 29th of December dawned, and York sent out some patrols to try to gather some food for his starving army. These patrols, despite the truce, (which may or may not have been arranged) were attacked by the Lancastrian forces to the north of Sandal.

York, furious at this, ordered his army to march out of Sandal, and to advance north, to where the parkland now is. There is a rumour that Queen Margaret made York march out to meet her by taunting his cowardice, a story which has found its way into Shakespeare's plays and some modern history books. This was not possible as she was in Berwick at the time trying to sell the city to the Scots. This is an example of how, even the greatest minds, are prepared to permit a good story overcome accurate history.

York must have been well aware, that he was outnumbered when he marched out, since the Lancastrian force would have been all too visible from the walls of Sandal. Why on earth did York, who had with him some very experienced captains, march out to fight a superior army?

Perhaps about the same time York saw the foraging party he had sent out to gather food being attacked, Lord Neville, the sprig of family to whom Salisbury belonged, appeared to the north, behind the forces of the Lancastrians. York, who may have received a signal from Neville about the time he was to make an entrance, understandably concluded that Neville would attack the Lancastrian forces in the rear.

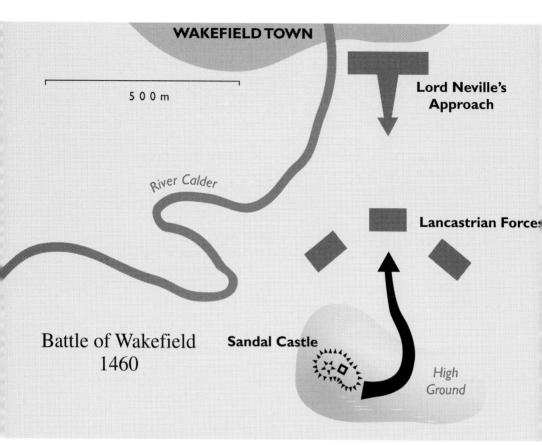

WAKEFIELD TOWN

500 m

Lord Neville's Approach

River Calder

Lancastrian Forces

Battle of Wakefield
1460

Sandal Castle

High Ground

Believing that he had the Lancastrians to rights, York marched out to meet the enemy and aid his foragers. And Lord Neville, in the rear of the Lancastrian army, did nothing. As so often in the Wars of the Roses, treachery did its deadly work.

York marched on to the Lancastrian army, which must have outnumbered him by at least five to one, and was engulfed by them. As his force was surrounded and was being cut to pieces York must have realised that he had been fooled. The treachery of Neville, and the attack on the Yorkist patrols forcing York to fight, could only have been arranged by Trollope of Calais, as the deftness of touch required to bring these actions together, bespeak the hand of a subtle and intelligent man.

Caught like a 'fish in net', the Yorkist army, we are told, was shattered in half an hour. As the Lancastrian army was about 12,000 men strong, the Yorkist army could not have been much over 2,000 strong in order for the defeat to be as quick as that. York it appears was cut down almost straight away, Salisbury was captured by the exultant Lancastrians, together with several other Yorkist leaders.

An interesting incident now occurred: Edmund, the Earl of Rutland, the Duke of York's son, managed to escape the slaughter, and flee to the chantry church on Wakefield Bridge. He was there overtaken by John, Lord Clifford, one of the most ruthless of the Lancastrian leaders, whose father had been killed at St Albans.

Rutland, it is said, cried for mercy, to which Clifford is reputed to have replied, 'Your father killed mine, so I will kill you and all your kin.' Later historians (especially the Victorians, needless to say) seem to think that Rutland was a young boy murdered by a vile animal in human form. As a matter of fact, Rutland was seventeen years of age, old enough to bear arms in those days (and in our time as a matter of fact), whom, as Phil Haigh points out, may have fought his way out of the battle itself.

The execution of Rutland by Clifford, occurred in a pursuit of a beaten army when anyone is fair game, and as the laws of the vendetta were now extant in the land, Clifford's hitman-like attitude, would not have been in any way strange. What is strange, is how on earth did Rutland get on the bridge in the first place? The bridge is to the north of the battle, and to get there he would have had to cut his way through the whole Lancastrian force. Would not running from the battle, that is, to the south have been more prudent?

Whatever the complexities of Rutland's death, what happened next was, to a degree, inevitable. The nobles of the Yorkist army, who had not been killed in the battle, including Salisbury and John Harrow, a captain of the army, were taken to Pontefract castle. The fate of the imprisoned at that establishment was not bright as both Richard II and Thomas of Lancaster had be incarcerated their and had lost their heads.

It was arranged that Salisbury, being a great nobleman, would be ransomed; the commons of Yorkshire however, had a different idea. A mob broke into the castle, took Salisbury out and beheaded him. It was stated afterwards, that the commons of the area 'loved Salisbury not'. As the majority of the commons at this stage, would not have had a clue as to the reasons their betters were killing each other, we can only conclude that the reason for Salisbury's 'lynching' by a rural proletariat, was that he was either a harsh landlord (the Nevilles had a lot of land in the area), or that he was regarded as being a very evil man.

The prisoners taken after the battle, were, if they were noble, summarily executed. The heads of Salisbury, Rutland and the Duke of York, were taken to the City of York, and placed over the top of Micklegate Bar. As a final insult to York's royal claims, a paper crown was put on his head, to mock the man who had tried so hard to come to some sort of agreement with his Royal master, but as a result of his lack of judgement and the treachery of his foes, had thrown the iron dice and lost.

The battle at Wakefield had wiped out almost all the older generation of the Yorkist leaders. The new Yorkist leader was Edward of March, now recruiting troops on the Welsh march.

Edward must have heard of the catastrophe at Wakefield quite soon, since it was said he was actually marching to London to aid Warwick when he heard that the Lancastrian Earls of Pembroke and Wiltshire were marching on Ludlow with the intention of invading the midlands via the River Severn.

Edward, in a burst of energy which was to be his hallmark throughout his life when faced with a crisis,

The heads of Richard, Duke of York, and his supporters adorning Micklegate Bar following the Yorkists' defeat at the Battle of Wakefield.

turned around, marched north, and, on 2nd February, at Mortimer's Cross near Ludlow, completely smashed the Lancastrian force. As revenge for the death of his father and brother, the leading nobles captured were beheaded in Hereford. One of the unlucky ones was

Northeast side of Sandal Castle, Wakefield.   By courtesy of Wakefield Historical Publications

View from Sandal Castle mound looking north west towards Wakefield.

The Chantry Bridge over the Calder at Wakefield. It was here that Lord Clifford slew young Edmund, the son of Richard Duke of York.

Detail of the figure of Richard Duke of York from the Victorian monument marking his death at the Battle of Wakefield (left), based on the original statue once on the Welsh Bridge at Shrewsbury.

Owen Tudor, a rather strange creature, who had married Catherine of France, the widow of the murderous Henry V, and so helped create the future Tudor dynasty.

Edward immediately began to march on London, since the news from the north was desperate. The Lancastrian forces, now joined by the spirited Queen Margaret, Henry VI, and her son, Edward Prince of Wales, with a pack of Peers, Northumberland, Somerset, Clifford and the irrepressible Andrew Trollop, cock-a-hoop after the battle of Wakefield, led their affinities south on a march to London.

Queen Margaret, who did not appear to have learned much about English sensibilities in the years since she became queen, allowed her army, which contained it seems a great many Scottish mercenaries and border ruffians, in lieu of pay, to ravage all England south of the Trent.

The ensuing episode, is one of the most famous incidents of the Wars of the Roses, and shows really, just how peaceful England was during this period, as such an incident would have been regarded as a fact on life in most areas of the Continent of Europe at that time.

After making a brief detour to pillage the town of Beverley, the Lancastrian army, swept down 'like a whirlwind', in the vivid and terrified metaphor of one contemporary, through the Midlands. The towns of Grantham, Stamford and Peterborough, were pillaged, the Lancastrian horde, advancing on a front of thirty miles caused terror wherever it went.

In London, pandemonium reigned. Warwick had organised such an effective propaganda campaign, that all in the city and the environs, were in fear of being killed or robbed by the northern hordes. This was an effort by Warwick to strengthen the resolve of the city to fight the Lancastrian army. To a degree however, this trick backfired, as many of the local nobles, aghast at the information regarding the invasion, threw in their lot with the Lancastrians to save their estates!

Warwick, who seemed to have behaved in a very dilatory manner, marched out to meet Margaret and her army (it cannot be said to have been Henry's) at the head of a force which consisted, for the most part, of Londoners. The Lancastrians (most likely advised by Trollop) instead of marching straight on to the enemy in the 'civilised' and accepted manner, marched around the Yorkist force, and hit it on the flank. This, together with some inexplicable lethargy on the part of Warwick's scouts, and coupled with the fact that Warwick had stretched his army on a very long front which made it very difficult to reinforce any part of his army, the Lancastrians

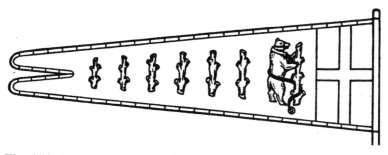

Warwick's standard depicting the bear and the ragged staff.

managed to put themselves on the flank of Warwick's force and roll it up. Warwick managed to extricate part of his army from the shambles, and proceeded to march west to find Edward, leaving a large number of men, together with his professional reputation behind him.

Margaret led her troops almost to the walls of London, where the populace, terrified by the army heading towards them, managed to throw off their panic, and slam the gates of the city in her face. Margaret had no choice but to withdraw slowly northwards, her army having been seriously thinned by desertions, for most of the Scottish and northerners, having plundered to their heart's content, left their anointed Sovereign and lord, in the time honoured manner of those days of honour and chivalry and run off home.

CHAPTER XIII

The Battle of Towton 1461

The Battle of Towton would prove to be the 'showdown' of the Wars of the Roses – the mediaeval equivalent to the fight at the OK Coral. With the deaths of York and Salisbury, Edward of March and Richard of Warwick, were now the heads of their family affinities. After having met up with Edward near Oxford, Warwick most likely put into Edward's head an idea which may have been germinating in both of their minds for a long time: as Edward was now the head of the family of York, and as there was no turning back now, why not proclaim Edward king?

Edward, Earl of March, became Edward IV – this in opposition to the then monarch, Henry VI. Two rival kings – the scene was set for an almighty battle.

The two Earls, March and Warwick, rode into London at the end of February to the wild enthusiasm of the populace. On the 1st of March, at Clerkenwell field, an interesting example of a rent-a-crowd occured. George Neville, a younger and rather glib brother of Warwick, the Chancellor of England, (a position from which he would be demoted in circumstances which were both humiliating and hilarious several years later) and Bishop of Exeter (a title which he had assumed at the age of twenty-two, several years below the age necessary to warrant that rank) asked the crowd, if Henry VI was worthy to remain king, and, if not, should Edward of March be the new ruler.

To the surprise of no one, Edward's rent-a-crowd agreed to Edward's appointment. A few weeks' short of his nineteenth birthday, Edward, the Earl of March, was thus pronounced king of England, by the Grace of God, his army, the machinations of Warwick, his kid brother George, and the plaudits of the populace of London. What else was needed?

Edward immediately set to work to raise more troops in order to march north and claim his kingdom by right of battle (then, as now, by far the most solid way of becoming a ruler). A veritable barrage of writs and commissions of array were despatched to the shires and towns of the kingdom. The Yorkist captains were despatched to their own shires to recruit as many troops as possible, while Edward managed to persuade the council of London, to give him over £4,000 to pay his troops and to purchase provisions. Edward had realised the affect which the plundering of Margaret's troops had had on the political psyche, and was determined not to repeat the same mistake.

George, third son of Richard of York, supporter of his elder brother Edward as king. He would later turn against his brother and end up in the Tower of London where he is believed to have been drowned in a barrel of Malmesy wine.

When the Yorkist contingents began to concentrate and march to the north, the sheer size of the armies commanded by both sides would show just how much importance the political establishment attached to the inevitable clash of arms. Edward had published a list of rewards for anyone who killed named enemies of the house of York – upon which list Andrew Trollope was a most prominent entry.

With Edward marched the Earl of Warwick, the Duke of Norfolk, the Earl of Arundel and a pack a lesser peers and knights. To the north, near York, which, to the distress of its inhabitants, would once again be a staging ground for slaughter, Queen Margaret would have with her the armies of the Dukes of Somerset and Exeter, the Earls of Wiltshire, Devon and Northumberland, and the men of Lords Clifford, Roos and a huge group of knights and gentry. Given the numbers of nobility and gentry attached to both armies, we can only assume that most of the adult peerage, and a quite unprecedented number of knights and gentry were squaring up for an event which would sort this matter out once and for all.

They were not to be disappointed.

With reference to the battle itself (perhaps Hecatomb would be a better word), not a lot is known about the slaughter at Towton. The most important writings being the following: Edward Hall, a historian writing almost a century after the event; Polydore Vergil, who most likely did not speak to anyone from the noble class (the literate class who would write the letters describing the combat); Jean de Waurin, an experienced professional courtier of the Duke of Burgundy, who got most of his information from the Earl of Warwick, who would prove to be a very unreliable source; and some letters written after the event by individuals who were not present at the battle, and depended on second or third hand information for their writings.

The Yorkist army marched north, with Nottingham being the agreed concentration point. The various bodies of the Yorkists, met here on the 22nd March. The decision was taken to march north, even though the Duke of Norfolk had not yet arrived with his troops. Pausing on their way only to allow Warwick to execute the bastard of Exeter at Coventry, who, for some unfathomable reason had not joined the Lancastrian force, the Yorkists reached Pontefract on 27th March, where Warwick's father had been executed only a few weeks before.

The Lancastrian force, less the devout Henry VI who, as more than one commentator has remarked, had been present at a remarkable degree of violence and bloodshed for such an ineffectual and peaceful man, marched out of the City of York to meet their foes, past the grinning bird-pecked heads of Richard and his followers

Micklegate Bar, York, the mediaeval display place for grisly trophies of the Wars of the Roses – severed human heads.

The now defunct bridge at Ferrybridge where a clash of arms took place in March 1461. Lord Clifford, for the Lancastrians, had occupied the nearside bank after breaking the then wooden structure across the Aire. A constant flurry of arrows showered into the Yorkists as they attempted a repair.

on Micklegate Bar. A gap had apparently been left between them for the head of Edward Earl of March to take up its place there.

The Lancastrians took up position on the undulating countryside around the small village of Towton, and sent out scouts to the south to observe the Yorkist approach.

On 28th March, 1461, the first bloodshed would occur, at Ferrybridge, the main crossing point of the River Aire. This was the river the Yorkists would have to cross in order to come to grips with their foes. Given the fact that the winter snows must have swelled the river, like the Ure at Boroughbridge, it must have presented a formidable obstacle. It also appears to have been destroyed by the Lancastrians on their withdrawal north from London.

Edward promptly ordered the bridge to be repaired, under the oversight of Lord Fitzwalter. The repair was indeed carried out, but Fitzwalter would not rate much kudos for his efforts. After completing the repairs, he and his men took to their beds for the night. He received a rude awakening when Lord Clifford, the executioner of the young Earl of Rutland at Wakefield Bridge, rode at the head of a raiding party and attacked the Yorkist camp on the north bank of the river.

What happened next is open to some disagreement. According to the Chronicler Hall, the Earl of Warwick, on hearing of the attack, rode to Edward at Pontefract where he informed the King of the setback, and then slaughtered his horse saying he would not take a step back, and he who wished to, could flee the field. This is rather too good a story to have been made up. Warwick's somewhat hysterical reaction to the raid at Ferrybridge, may well have soured Edward in his view of his cousin.

Edward sounded the alarm, and it seems, sent out a section of his army under Lord Fauconberg, (Warwick's uncle), with orders to pass over the Aire at Castleford and take the Lancastrians in the flank.

While Fauconberg rode to the east, Edward marched to Ferrybridge with the rest of his army, where a bewildering incident took place. We are told by Waurin, that a great battle was fought at Ferrybridge, and that the Yorkists, aided by the efforts of Lord Fauconberg, who had ridden over the ford at Castleford, and was now marching to the east, threatening Clifford's retreat to the north.

Clifford, we are told, realising the predicament that he was in, ordered a withdrawal to the Lancastrian main force at Towton. In the ride to the north, Clifford's party, which included the turncoat Lord Neville the betrayer of the Duke of York during the Battle of Wakefield, was intercepted and ambushed by a mounted contingent of Lord Fauconberg's men. Clifford, Neville and most of his party were slaughtered that night, in Dintingdale Valley, only a short distance from the main Lancastrian force. Clifford taking an arrow in the throat, as a result of taking off his gorget (neck protection) during a brief halt.

Why didn't help for Lord Clifford's raiding party materialise from the Lancastrian main force gathering in strength a short distance from the ambush site?

And at Ferrybridge: If Clifford had intended to make a serious stand at that crossing point of the River Aire, it would have been necessary for him to have been reinforced in strength. It should be pointed out that Ferrybridge was almost ten miles to the south of the main position of the Lancastrians. On the other hand, if the action of Clifford was intended as a delaying operation why did he hang about after causing havouc among Fitzwalter's bridging party? He should have got away from the area upon completion of the raid.

This author can only conclude that either Clifford, in his

impetuosity, stayed at Ferrybridge far longer than was necessary, or that Fauconberg had been sent to take part of the army around Castleford far sooner than has been given credence; on the other hand it is possible that the action of Clifford, and his subsequent death in Dintingdale Valley, resulted from a mix-up in the plans of the Lancastrians who, unlike the Yorkists under Edward IV, had no natural leader. Henry VI was totally ineffectual and Somerset did not having a large enough affinity of men to warrant his being given overall command of the Lancastrian army. This leads to the conclusion that the main generals were the Lords Clifford and Northumberland, Trollope being a mere knight, and in those status conscious days, not having the weight in the counsel chamber, despite being easily the best commander.

Further, Northumberland and Clifford it seems were natural rivals for leadership, both having a lot to prove to avenge their fathers. This author is of the opinion that Clifford may have led the raid on his own initiative, and expected some help to come to him on the retreat. Confusion could have occured in the Lancastrian councils, as to what appropriate action to take in the light of the success of the raid and the subsequent withdrawal. Clifford was killed in a pretty needless fashion. The lack of support he got throughout that day, as he seriously hindered the Yorkist forces at the River Aire crossing, did not augur well for the fortunes on the morrow for the Lancastrian main force.

Following the capture of the bridge, we are told by Waurin, the not-very-well informed Burgundian, that the whole of the army passed over the bridge in one night, a logistical impossibility, as we can state that at least 15,000 men, would have to cross over a very narrow bridge and be up at the fields near Towton, ten miles away by the morning of the 29th. We are left with the conclusion, that the force sent by Edward under Fauconberg, was a good deal larger than has been imagined, and that the Yorkists crossed over the River Aire in two places, Castleford and Ferrybridge, not one.

Whatever happened, it is certain that the Yorkists were in position just to the north of Saxton village, a hamlet two miles to the south of Towton, in the morning of the 29th. Both sides of must have been cursing the weather, as it was cold, windy and snowing, the snow giving a romantic picture to a scene which would now be the place of perhaps the most appalling slaughter in the history of the English nation.

Given the great numbers of Lords and peers present at the battle, even cynical historians have agreed the numbers engaged must have

St Mary's Chapel, Lead. This was once the site of a small settlement (houses all gone) and is a mile behind the Yorkist positions. It must have been the case that soldiers sought shelter here before, during and after the battle of Towton.

been huge. It is agreed that the Lancastrians must have started the battle with about 25,000 plus men and the Yorkists, with approximately 20,000, with the Duke of Norfolk's 5,000 men, still on the way from Pontefract.

Little is known of the actual line up of the two armies, but we can agree that Edward and Warwick, with Fauconberg helping them, were the commanders of the Yorkist force and that Somerset, Northumberland and Trollop were the commanders of their foes. The exact divisions of each army is also not known, though according to the unreliable Waurin, Somerset commanded the right hand battle of the Lancastrians, and Northumberland the left hand battle. The confusion to be found surrounding the incident of lack of support for Clifford by the Lancastrian high command, would rear its head again.

Given the enormous size of both armies, with men being shoved into position, captains conferring between themselves and the

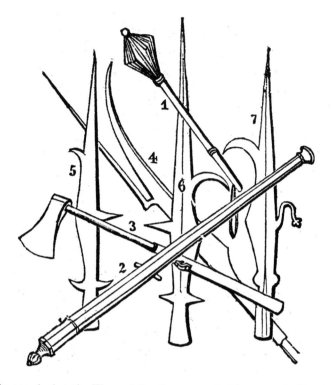

Weapons in use during the Wars of the Roses: 1. Mace;   2. Hand-cannon;
3. Combined hand-gun and battle-axe;   4. Guisarme;   5,6,7. Various types of Bills.

inevitable disorder, it cannot have been before nine in the morning that the two armies were ready to begin the slaughter. To add to the interest in the proceedings, the wind which we are given to understand had been blowing from the north, had swund round to blow from the south, sending flurries of snow directly into the faces of the Lancastrians. This storm was making it almost impossible for both armies to see each other. It is from this occurance that one of the few facts about the battle emerges.

According to the Tudor Chronicler, Hall, the leader of the Yorkist first line, ordered his archers to march forward, shoot one volley of arrows into the Lancastrian ranks, then fall back. The wind, carrying the arrows, caused the missiles to make the distance and fall among the ranks of the Lancastrians. As at least 10,000 of the Yorkists were archers, that sudden wooden shower shrouded in and accompanying the snow storm, must have come as a terrible shock.

The Lancastrians replied immediately and their archers let fly their shafts in return. However, the wind was now blowing ferociously in their faces, and their arrows fell short by '40 Tailors Yards'.

The Lancastrians it seems, continued to fire for several minutes, till many of the archers had spent their arrows. When the arrow storm seemed to be abating, Fauconberg, ordered his men to march forward and to collect the arrows, now littering the battlefield. With their quivers now stocked with shafts, the Yorkists, proceeded to loose flight after flight of arrows into the Lancastrian ranks.

With at least 10,000 archers pouring their arrows into their ranks, the situation, as put pithily by Andrew Boardman, must have 'resembled a Turkey shoot', the casualties must have been severe on the Lancastrian side, whose leaders decided that they had no choice but to advance against the Yorkists so as to put an end to the casualties being caused by the Yorkist archers. Consequently, at about 10 am, the Lancastrian lines began to surge forward, under the banners of Somerset, Northumberland, Exeter and the northern lords. The Lancastrian iron wall was on the move in order to come under the arrow hail.

The chronicler, Waurin tells us, that Somerset led one wing of the army, and Northumberland the other. As he wrote his history after about 1465, when all the Lancastrian leaders were dead or in exile, and his only source for this affair, was the very unreliable Earl of Warwick, we cannot come to any conclusion as to who led which part of the Lancastrian host.

The two armies clashed on a frontage of about one mile, and for the next few hours England saw a battle of savagery and brutality which for the numbers involved and the continuous action, had no parallel in her history. Dukes, Earls, Lords,

How the men of means fought their battles during the Wars of the Roses. An extremely expensive metal suit.

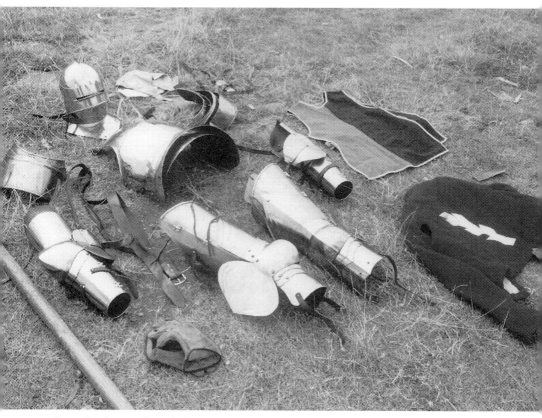

Reproduction medieaval plate armour suit laid out on display following a battle re-enactment at the Royal Armouries, Leeds. This faithfully copied armour and livery represents a knight in the service of the Earl of Warwick – note the ragged staff motive sown on the doublet.

knights, archers and footmen, grappled and killed with a blood lust about which all the chroniclers agree. Edward himself, a giant killing machine at 6′4″ tall, encased in armour, vowed to die with his soldiers rather than flee this day and, by all accounts, did terrible execution with his own hand.

There is an interesting vignette regarding this slaughter: the Lancastrian, Lord Dacre, while taking off his helmet to get some air, was killed (purportedly) by a boy with a crossbow, who had stationed himself in an elderberry tree. Apparently the lad had recognised Dacre as the killer of his father. How he could have seen him in a snowstorm, amidst some 30,000 men all thrashing about has caused many of the more cynical historians to doubt this story. Some historians, following Waurin, claim that part of the Lancastrians managed to force the left wing of the Yorkists to give ground, and that Edward himself with his household men, came forward to steady the line and slaughter all before him.

As Waurin's sources were only the Earl of Warwick and perhaps, churchmen who had never been to the combat, this story must be treated with some caution. The fact that Edward, with his great stamina, height and skill at arms, visited parts of the field to assist where the Yorkist line was most pressed, inspiring his men by his presence, is not to be doubted at all.

The most reliable account of Towton, comes from the dispassionate and careful Italian historian Vergil, who writes

'for ten hours the fight continued in equal balance, when at last King Henry [read Somerset, most likely, for this] *espied the forces*

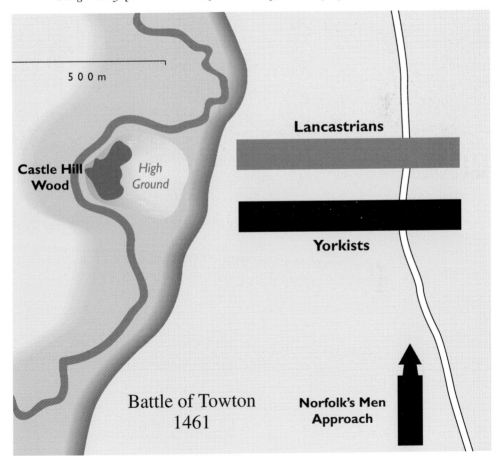

Battle of Towton
1461

Effigy of Yorkist leader the Earl of Warwick depicting his likely dress for the Battle of Towton.

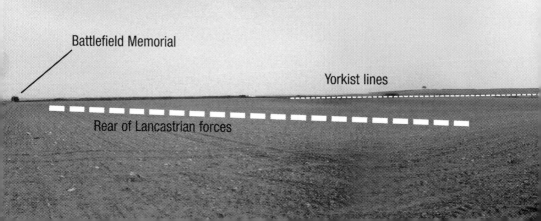

Battlefield Memorial

Yorkist lines

Rear of Lancastrian forces

of his foes increase and his own somewhat yield, when by new exhortation he had compelled to press on more earnestly, he with a few horsemen, removing a little out of the place, expected the event of the fight, but behold, suddenly his soldiers gave the back, which when he saw this he fled also.'

Here we have the answer to what happened at Towton: for ten hours, both sides had been slaughtering each other, each side must have been reaching the end of its physical and mental stamina. The force of the Duke of Norfolk, suddenly appeared on the field, most likely at the right wing of the Yorkists. The sight of the new soldiers must have had a demoralising effect on the Lancastrians who, not surprisingly, began to buckle under the strain of the fresh attack. The Duke of Somerset, from Vergil's passage, certainly fell back a little at the sight of Norfolk's men. The Lancastrian force, most likely starting from the eastern flank, began to fall back; starting in ones and two's, then in scores, than by the hundreds, the Lancastrians fell back. An army, which had fought ferociously for about 10 hours, began to disintegrate, as a result of reinforcement coming at the right physical and mental moment. Within under a quarter of an hour, in this author's opinion, the Lancastrian line was broken and in route. All discipline ceased as they tried to get away from the now triumphant Yorkists.

Where they met their nemesis

The battlefield of Towton is bounded on its western side by the narrow Cock River which, as it was then a raging torrent because of the meltwater snows flooding into it, was a deep and narrow channel. As the road to York, the Ferrybridge Tadcaster road, was now held by the men of Norfolk, the Lancastrians had to flee to the north and north west, by way of the steep valley of the river Cock and cross its flooded and raging waters.

As the Lancastrians ran to the edge of the slope leading to the

A view of the battlefield taken from a location behind where the Lancastrian forces would have stood and from where an information board stands today.

Bloody Meadow   Castle Hill Wood

The Lancastrians broke and fled the field of carnage down into this valley. Pursuing Yorkist troops carried out a great slaughter down these slopes. The Cock Beck was a raging torrent at the time of the battle and formed a barrier to the fleeing troops.

A tranquil scene in 2001 as a rustic bridge crosses the Cock Beck. This was once the London Road which climbed up the valley side to Tadcaster. On Palm Sunday, 29th March 1461, a mass of terrified men would have been pressing towards you across a similiar wooden construction pursued by victorious Yorkists. The water would have been filled with struggling, desperate men clambering over each other in panic in attempts to avoid the slashing axes, maces and swords. There are reports of 'bridges of bodies' and the water running red with blood as the rout of the vanquished stretched on up to Tadcaster and towards York itself.

Cock, some must have been aghast at the sight of the waters they had to somehow cross. Panic-stricken colleagues would most likely have then shoved them down the slope. The flood of soldiers, slipping and sliding down the slope towards the waters of the Cock, must have presented a terrible sight. As more and more fleeing men poured down the slopes, those at the front would have been thrown into the river. So great were the numbers of the Lancastrians crossing the Cock, that it was stated that some of them were able to cross dry-shod over the river on the corpses of their drowned colleagues. Given the width and depth of the river at that time of year, the numbers that died in the icy river, must have run into the thousands.

The lucky few of the Lancastrians, who had retreated up the Tadcaster road before the men of Norfolk cut it, left behind a field of appalling carnage. Over an area of two square miles some 20,000 men lay dead or dying on the field, or piled up in the River Cock. The chronicles agree that both sides had declared that was to be no quarter given for this battle. Those who fell wounded but not dead, would by the time the sun had set have their throats slit with 'Bollack' daggers.

The casualties on that day, on a pro rata basis, would be far worse than any other battle fought by the English. At least 0.8% of the whole English population being killed or wounded in one day.

The night drew in, with the snow still falling, the dead and wounded of both sides being plundered of their belongings in the time-honoured fashion of warfare. Whilst this was going on some of the Yorkist army, advanced north to Tadcaster on the heels of the escapees to kill any stragglers they caught up with.

At least 20,000 Lancastrians, and 8,000 Yorkists died on that terrible day. Over the two days fighting, the losses in the ruling class had been appalling; on the Yorkist side, only Lord Fitzwalter and the unscrupulous Kentish captain

Now it was the turn of the Lancastrian leaders to lose their heads and have them decorate the walls of the City of York.

The tomb of Lord Dacre, killed in the Battle of Towton, in Saxton churchyard.

Robert Horne had been killed. In the Lancastrian ranks however, the slaughter was terrible; five peers had died in battle: Clifford; Lord Neville, the traitor of Wakefield; Northumberland and Lords Dacre and Wells. The Earl of Devon, was captured in York, too ill to move.

A few days later, his head replaced that of Richard Duke of York, his son Earl of Rutland and other Yorkists on Micklegate Bar. Sir Andrew Trollope, the dashing Captain of Calais, was also killed, dying as violently and sensationally as he had lived. Over 40 knights were killed in that appaling battle.

Whatever the losses, Towton, is probably the most ferocious battle to ever have been fought on English soil.

What were the results of this hecatomb?

Firstly, Edward would prove himself to be the strong man of England, and Towton would be the keystone of his success. Though Edward would later have to fight and kill Warwick, the confiscations of property, together with eradication of many of his enemies, would enable Edward to construct a governing apparatus, built on the power of the crown, the like of which still had to be found in Europe. This centralised monarchy would, under Henry VIII and Elizabeth, enable England to develop a new religion, a centralised state, and become a power in the world.

And a lot of the credit lies with the fallen warriors at Towton.

TRAVELLER'S GUIDE TO THE BATTLEFIELDS OF YORKSHIRE

Brunanburh 937 AD

Virtually the entire site of the battlefield of Brunnanburh is now built over. This battleground does not have a monument to aid the visitor. Those wishing the explore the area are advised to travel to the Meadowhall shopping complex close to motorway M1 exits 33 and 34. Also it can be reached by rail or National Express coach services. From Meadowhall a 222 bus will take you to Sheffield City Airport. Upon reaching the airport enter the car park and look towards the northeast. You will see the Tinsley marshalling yards over which most of the conflict raged.

At a more grass roots level a number 221 bus from the main bus stations at Rotherham or Sheffield will take you to Brinsworth Road. Leaving the bus between Brinsworth and Catcliffe, the vistor will be able to get a feel of the lay of the land over which the battle was fought. However, be warned, unlike some of the Yorkshire battlefields such as Byland or Towton, the industrialized nature of the area makes any totally accurate orientation problematic.

Gate Fulford, York, 1066

Like Brunnanburh, this area is now almost completely urbanized making it difficult to define what the site of the battle was like at the time. It is suggested that the visitor walk along the southern circuit of the walls of York. This is a good vantage point to observe where the Saxon army advanced to meet the Norwegian host. By passing through what remains of the Fish Gate, which can be approached by walking down Piccadilly. This is the road used by the Saxons on their way out of the City to do battle. Orientation is problematic.

Stamford Bridge, 1066

The appraoches to this site are more interesting than the site itself. By catching a number 10 bus on Rougier Street in York, the visitor will be travelling along the route which the army of King Harold took to fight the invading Nordsmen in 1066. It is recommended that the visitor leave the bus at Gate Helmsley, one and three quarter miles from Stamford Bridge. From here the visitor will observe the pronounced contours of the area, which makes clear how the Saxon army was able to march so close to the enemy during their advance towards the army Hardrada without being observed.

Northallerton, 1138

There is a regular train service to Northallerton from where the visitor can reach the battlefield by local bus, taxi or on foot. The battlefield is less than three miles to the north. Travellers by car coming from the either the north or south should take the A167, which runs through the centre of the area of the battlefield. Although there is a monument about three miles to the north of the town, it is largely a matter of conjecture as to the exact place of the fight.

Myton-on-Swale, 1319

Like the Towton battlefield this is also largely an unspoiled area. There are no railways nearby and this author has been unable to find any coach companies with regular routes passing close to the village. A car is therefore essential in order to visit this battlefield site. The visitor should drive along the A19 until the road signs signal the turn-off for Tollerton village. Continue through Flawith to the village of Myton – approximately six miles. Waterproof footwear is suggested for walking this site as the ground is low-lying.

Boroughbridge, 1322

This is another unspoilt area close to the banks of the River Ure. Travel to this area by car along the A1 (M). Turn off on to the B 6265, about one mile either north or south of the town. Follow the signs to the town centre of Boroughbridge. There is ample parking to the north of the river with a picnic area nearby. The bridge across the River Ure in the town centre stands approximately on the same site as the original bridge at the time of the battle, where the Earl of Lancaster was defeated.

Byland, 1322

Yet another unspoilt historic battlefield site. There are a number of bus and train services to Thirsk, which stands about five miles to the east of the battlefield. There are a number of bus service which run during the summer holiday period and these are best found out by ringing the bus services information line on: 0870 608 2608. Taxis are also available from Thirsk which will take you to the battlefield which lies on the escarpment of the Hambleton Hills. If you decide to walk from Thirsk along the A170 please beware that because of the curving road and hair-pin bends, drivers are restricted in their view of pedestrians. To the east of the battlefield are a number of cafes where visitors can refresh themselves after a climb up Sutton Bank. Once on top of the ridge where the A170 comes over the ridge is where it is believed the centre of the English line was located. Walk about 200 yards to the south. This is where the Scottish Islesmen and Highlanders are believed to have outflanked the English. The magnificent view to the west enables the visitor to appreciate the consternation the English force must have experienced when they saw the army of the Scots advancing to meet them.

Wakefield, 1460

This battlefield is accessible and relatively easy to visualize.
Visitors travelling by train should ensure that they arrive in
Wakefield at Wakefield Kirkgate station, not Westgate. On
leaving Kirkgate station travel west along Station Passage or
Calder Vale Road. After a short walk you will come out to
Kirkgate/Doncaster Road. Proceeding south you will come to
the bridges crossing the River Calder. Note the old, now
subsidiary bridge on which is the Chantry Chapel. This is
where young Edmund, Earl of Rutland, was killed by the
'Bloody' Clifford. After viewing this structure, part of which
stonework dates back to the time of the battle of Wakefield,
walk down Bridge Street/Barnsley Road for about half a mile
then turn right down Manygates Lane. This will eventually
bring you to the ruins of Sandal Castle.If travelling by bus then
a number of routes pass Sandal Castle. Ask to be let off at
Castle Grove Infirmary. From the stop walk along Pinfold Lane,
then Castle Road and Manygates Lane to the castle site itself.
Should you travel in by car by way of the M1 then leave the
motorway at junction 39 and join the A636 heading towards
Wakefield. Turn right at the first roundabout past Pugney's
Country Water Park and you will see Sandal Castle mound to
your left. Pass Asda store and continue to the traffic lights and
straight on to the castle.
Walk on the path to the north of the ruin and looking due north
you will be rewarded by a panoramic view of what some
consider to be the battlefield. Be warned that the slopes of the
castle mound are extremely slippery at certain times and
strong shoes (and sound heart) are required to make the climb.
Should you wish to visit the site where Richard Duke of York
made his final stand with his back to three trees, walk from the
castle down Manygates Lane and when you come to a school-
like building on the left you will see the monument.

A Visitor Centre will be opening in summer 2002.

Manygates Lane, off Barnsley Road, Wakefield
Telephone enquiries to: 01924 305352
Castle opening times: Daily dawn to dusk (Car park 9.30
am to dusk)

Towton, 1461

This is perhaps the most unspoiled battlefield described in this book. Visitors travelling by bus from Leeds or York need the Coastliner service to Tadcaster, which runs every half hour. From Tadcaster take the Pontefract bus, which runs every one to two hours, and get off at Towton village. From the village it is about one mile along the B1217 to the battlefield monument. The visitor is advised to check with bus service information on: 0870 608 2608, for up-to-date service information. For the rail traveller there are stops at Church Fenton and Ulleskelf. From both stops it is roughly two miles to the battlefield – in both cases on lightly used country roads.

By car from the A1 leave at junction 48 on the new motorway-standard section and join the B1217, which is signposted Lotherton Hall. Drive past the hall and on to the Crooked Billet public house, on the right. You are now in the rear of the Yorkist forces. A mile further on you will come to the memorial on your left where you can park off the road. Walk along the footpath across the field to where the hedge line is and you will see a battlefield explanation board placed there by the Towton Battlefield Society. Down the steep slope you will see the Cock Beck meandering along the valley. It was down this slope that the broken Lancastrian rabble streamed to avoid the steel of the Yorkists.

Go down into Towton and the Rockingham Arms where a good meal may be had. There are numerous items on display which relate to the bloody battle which took place just up the road over five hundred years ago. Down the side of the pub car park is the old London Road – now a mere cart track. Follow this until you reach Slaughter Bridge over the Cock. Perhaps stand on the bridge, half close your eyes and imagine the incredible carnage which took place at this spot – by far the bloodiest battle ever to have been fought in this country.

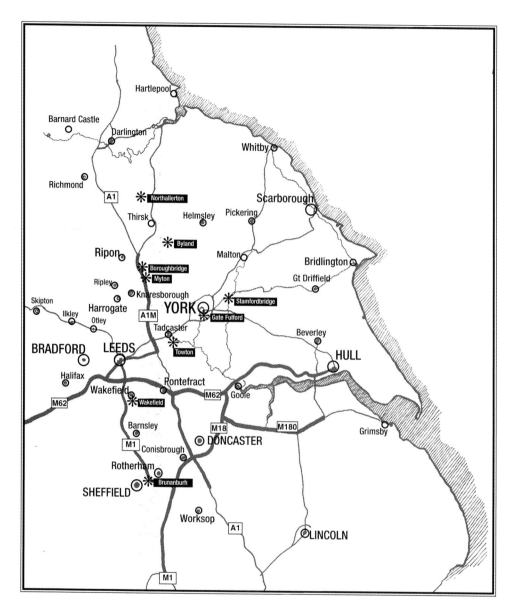

Hartlepool

Barnard Castle
Darlington

Whitby

Richmond

A1 ✳ Northallerton

Scarborough

Thirsk   Helmsley   Pickering

✳ Byland

Ripon   Malton   Bridlington

Boroughbridge   Gt Driffield

Ripley   ↓ Myton
Knaresborough

Skipton   ✳ Stamfordbridge

Harrogate   YORK
Ilkley   Otley   A1M   Gate Fulford

Tadcaster   Beverley

BRADFORD   LEEDS   ✳ Towton   HULL

Halifax   Pontefract
Wakefield   M62   Goole
M62   ✳ Wakefield

Barnsley   M18   M180
M1   Conisbrough   DONCASTER   Grimsby

Rotherham   ✳ Brunanburh
SHEFFIELD

Worksop   A1   ◉ LINCOLN

M1

ANGLO-SAXON CALENDAR

A Saxon Blacksmith.—From an old MS.

Among the best documents for information on former times and customs are ancient calendars. Twelve illustrations, each depicting a month of the year, composed some time prior to the Norman invasion serve to familiarize the reader with what life was like in and around Yorkshire some fifteen hundred years ago.

JANUARY   The heathen Saxons called this month 'Wolf-month' because the wolves were at their most ravenous. It was also called 'Aefter Yula' (after Christmas). Oxen are being used to draw the plough.

FEBRUARY   They called this the 'Cake Month' an allusion to the cakes offered to the gods. The pancake-making custom for Shrove Tuesday is an echo of this pagan practice. Trees are being cut for firewood.

MARCH   Dedicated to the goddess Rhoeda and called 'Rhed-monath', also called 'Illd-monath' (stormy month). They are seen to be digging, hoeing and sowing with some gusto.

APRIL   Month of the goddess Eustre (Easter). The men are seen here quaffing ale from drinking horns in celebration of the birth of Spring. Chairs and sofas were not then used by the Saxons and the figures are depicted sitting on ornate benches. Note the figure on guard duty.

MAY　　　　Called 'Trimilki' because they were able to milk the animals three times a day. May-day was the great rural festival celebrated with pomp and rejoicing. Sheperds are watching over ewes and lambs.

JUNE　　　　Referred to as 'Weyd-monath' because of the inclination of cattle to head into the marshes at this time. Also 'Mid-summer' month, when Saxons tended to take to the sea; they are depicted cutting wood for that purpose.

JULY　　　　'Hen-monath' (foliage month), also called 'Hey-monath' (hay month) the time for mowing and hay-making. It was also called 'Lida-aftera' (second lida), or the month following the month with the longest day.

AUGUST　　　　Called by the Saxons 'Arn-monath' or 'Barn-monath' (harvest month). The man with the horn and spear could well be a watchman on hand to warn of any hostile incursion. Implements depicted are of a type still in use in the nineteenth century.

SEPTEMBER 'Gerst-monath' (barley month) named from the liquor produced at this time called beerlegh – hence 'barley'. The subject of the engraving is a boar hunt.

OCTOBER   'Cold-monath' or 'Wyn-monath (wine month). The grape vine was extensively cultivated in England during the time of the Saxons. The figures are engaged in hawking.

NOVEMBER   'Blod-monath' (blood month) because of the great number of cattle killed for winter stores – some as sacrifices to the deities. Great fires were lit in the open to honour the gods. Men are seen warming themselves.

DECEMBER 'Fust-' or 'Winter-monath' and after the arrival of Christianity 'Heilig' (holy). Christmas took the place of the feast for Thor and the wassail bowl of heavy drinking continued to be circulated, but no longer for the pagan god but supposedly to honour Christ. Corn is being threshed and winnowed with a fan – produce is being carried away.